Recruiting Excellence

"The complete recruitment source book: strategic, evidence-based, comprehensive and above all, focused on achieving results in today's world."

Gary Hoyte, Director, Gary Hoyte Consulting Ltd (former HR Director of Scope)

"This book, in a straightforward, practical and insightful way tells companies and hiring executives how to minimise the luck factor in recruiting excellence and maximise the process excellence."

Stewart Rogers, Managing Director, The Rogers Partnership Ltd.

"This really is a unique and genuinely practical guide to the art of recruiting."

John Archer, Partner, Archer Mathieson

"If you need help in the war for talent, look no further than this insider's guide."

Chris Tanner, Independent Company Director and Business Consultant (formerly director of Training at Deloitte & Touche)

"From board members downwards – everyone involved in deciding who works in your organisation should read this. It'll arm you well for the battles that need to be won in the war for talent."

Mark Ryes, former Director of Programmes, TV Jobshop

"A comprehensive and very readable guide to hiring people, to be kept on the bottom shelf for easy reference."

Des Gunewardena, Chief Executive, Conran Holdings

"Employers will save many thousands of pounds by utilising the ideas within this book – a real insider's guide to effective recruiting."

Mike Walmsley, Co-founder, Recruitment Training Productions Ltd.

Recruiting Excellence

An Insider's Guide to Sourcing Top Talent

Jeff Grout and Sarah Perrin

THE McGRAW-HILL COMPANIES

London · Burr Ridge IL · New York · St Louis · San Francisco · Auckland
Bogatá · Caracas · Lisbon · Madrid · Mexico · Milan
Montreal · New Delhi · Panama · Paris · San Juan · São Paulo
Singapore · Sydney · Tokyo · Toronto

Recruiting excellence: an insider's guide to sourcing top talent
Jeff Grout and Sarah Perrin

0077099680

Published by McGraw-Hill Professional

Shoppenhangers Road
Maidenhead
Berkshire
SL6 2QL
Telephone: 44 (0) 1628 502 500
Fax: 44 (0) 1628 770 224
Website: www.mcgraw-hill.co.uk

British Library Cataloguing in Publication Data
A catalogue record for this book is available from the British Library

Library of Congress Cataloguing in Publication Data
The Library of Congress data for this book is available from the Library
of Congress

Sponsoring Editor: Elizabeth Robinson
Editorial Assistant: Sarah Butler
Business Marketing Manager: Elizabeth McKeever
Senior Production Manager: Max Elvey
Production Editor: Eleanor Hayes

Produced for McGraw-Hill by Gray Publishing, Tunbridge Wells
Printed and bound in the UK by Bell and Bain, Glasgow
Cover design by Simon Levy Associates

McGraw-Hill books are available at special quantity discounts. Please
contact the Corporate Sales executive at the above address.

Contents

Foreword

People Are Your Powerhouse

People are your powerhouse. That is the fundamental principle that forms the basis of this book. Yet many organisations still struggle to attract, select and retain the kind of quality people they need to drive their operations forward. Whether a multinational public company, a public sector body, a mid-sized regional player or a local business, everyone faces similar challenges in finding the human resources (HR) they need.

The importance of having top-quality people is now well established. You can have systems and processes, knowledge banks and data warehouses, but if you do not have the people with the right behaviours to use that knowledge or to apply that knowledge, then you will never maximise your organisational performance.

The value of brain power

In their book, *Funky Business*, Swedish academics Kjell Nordström and Jodas Ridderstråle emphasise the importance of people power in terms of intellectual potential rather than physical bodies. 'Perfectly formed and individually owned, the human brain is overpowering the traditional means of production – raw material, hard labour and capital. Try to think of one major, successful contemporary business organization that is brawn-based.'[1]

Interest in brain power has been exacerbated by the modern business phenomenon whereby businesses with little in the way of hard, tangible assets are the ones that attract the highest stock market valuations. Microsoft. Need we say more?

Most of the value in such businesses lies in their intangible assets, such as know-how, cutting edge technology or brand values. Intellectual capital is a key subset of the intangible assets group.

'Intellectual capital is knowledge that can be converted to profits.' This definition, from management consultancy ICM, an expert in intellectual capital management, identifies three major components of intellectual capital: HR, intellectual assets, and intellectual property. HR provide know-how and skills, but they are also key to the development of intellectual assets (codified knowledge) and intellectual property (such as patents or trademarks). People, therefore, really do hold the key to generating value in the modern business.

As the importance of intangible assets has become evident, so attention has focused on how to measure them, and organisations' ability to manage them. Swedish academic Karl Erik Sveiby created an Intangible Assets Monitor in 1994, a format designed to both measure and present an organisation's performance in managing those assets. In his approach 'competence' formed one of the three intangible asset groups, focused on employee's ability in areas such as skill, education, experience, values and social skills. Skandia, the Swedish international savings and insurance group, took up the theory, adapting it slightly to produce its own Skandia Navigator. Skandia publishes intellectual capital supplements, including its latest navigator, twice a year. Swedish-based consultancy Celemi has also published an Intangible Assets Monitor since 1995. It formally measures its people in terms of growth and renewal (using measures of professional experience, for example), efficiency (including value-added per expert) and stability (using indicators such as a satisfaction index and turnover rates).

The value of recruiting excellence

Research by pay-and-benefits experts Watson Wyatt has shown how the quality of personnel impacts on corporate value. The firm has created a Human Capital Index – a single set of measures that quantifies exactly what HR practices and policies have the most effect on increasing or decreasing shareholder value.

Watson Wyatt conducted its initial Human Capital Index study in North America in 1999, repeating the research in Europe in 2000. Both studies found that excellence in recruiting increased shareholder value. Recruiting excellence was interpreted to mean effectively planned recruitment that supports the business plan by placing the right people with ready-to-use skills in the right roles. In Europe, recruiting excellence was found to increase a company's market value by 1.5%. Where labour markets are tightest, effective recruiting may have an even stronger impact on a company's market value.

Why this book?

Recruiting Excellence is intended for a variety of people: board-level executives considering the importance of people power for propelling their business forward; HR departments charged with implementing cutting-edge recruitment policies; and line managers trying to fit effective recruitment into an already over-burdened working schedule.

There are books that talk about the strategic importance of attracting and managing talented people. There are other publications that give practical advice on how to recruit effectively. This book combines the two. We wanted to present practical advice for successful recruitment in the context of the strategic imperative for organisations to be able to tap into the best talent. Without this understanding, recruitment will at best be mechanistic and at worst, ineffective.

This book has a number of key aims. First to explain, for anyone who has not yet realised it, and who is remarkably still in business, why recruiting top-quality people is so important.

And why it is so difficult.

This forms the first section of the book, The Strategic Environment, where we consider the business agenda – what modern organisations need from their relationships with employees, and how recruitment can help to create those relationships. We also review the candidate's agenda and the changing expectations of the 21st century workforce. Against this background we then consider the strategic approaches that recruiters need to consider, and act on, in order to maximise their chances of successful recruitment. Even if you have a recruitment need, that does not mean that potential employees need you; the importance of attracting potential recruits is perhaps the most overlooked part of the recruitment process.

We also offer suggestions for less traditional means of sourcing new recruits and even alternatives to recruitment if the talent wars get too tough. We then consider common ways in which recruitment often goes wrong, just in case anyone still thinks it is a simple process.

If you have an urgent recruitment need or you think you know all about the strategic importance of recruiting already, you may want to jump straight into Part II: Practical Recruiting. Here we get down to our second key aim – providing some practical advice on how to handle the nitty-gritty of recruitment.

We look at how to establish what you are really looking for and whether you really have a recruitment need at all. If you do, we give you guidance on how to manage the recruitment process and how to decide whether you need to use the external services of recruitment consultants. We look at how to make advertising more effective and offer some tips on how to spot what you are looking for from the CVs or completed application forms you receive as a result.

Then, once you have aroused the interest of the talent out there, how do you identify what is really right for you? Selection can take many forms, from a simple interview to a combination of different tests designed to identify current and future potential.

By the way, most people think they are good interviewers. Unfortunately, many of them are overestimating their ability. The majority of interviewers fail to really get under the prepared, presentational surface of their interviewee's skin. We look at techniques for honing in on evidence of past behaviours as the best means of identifying likely future actions.

Once you have made your preferred selection, you still have to bring your chosen ones on board, and try to make sure they are effective once they get there. In Part III: After Selection: Getting the Best from Recruits, we consider the potentially delicate process of making offers and negotiating the kinds of packages that will net the people you want. Then, once they have signed the contract, we look at how to make sure you maximise their chances of thriving in your organisation in the way you want them to. Effective induction and on-going re-recruitment are essential requirements to make sure that your initial attraction and selection processes are not wasted.

However, as some people enter through your doors, so others may need to be encouraged to leave. Poor performers can seriously damage not only your organisation's health, but also your chances of attracting the best of the best to join you. We consider how to let people go in a way that minimises the damage for them and you.

The recruitment challenge

We make no bones about recruitment being easy. It is not. Even acknowledged HR expert Dr Gareth Jones, formerly Director of HR and Internal Communications at the BBC and currently Visiting Professor at INSEAD, appreciates the difficulties: 'Recruiting is the hardest thing you can do. I reckon that par for the course is to get it right 50% of the time. If you achieve 70%, you are a star. I think I'm good at it, but everyone makes mistakes; and mistakes are bloody expensive. Anything you can do to get your average up has to be a good thing.'

In researching this book we have drawn on the experiences of many other experts in recruitment and talent management. By including their insights, which are scattered throughout the text, we aim to provide a wide-ranging view of today's recruiting challenge and the potential responses to it.

This book is designed to push up your average, whatever your starting point. If you, and your organisation, become recruiting stars as a result, so much the better.

Above all, we want to help you achieve excellence in your recruiting and so increase your chances of attracting excellent recruits.

Acknowledgements

We are indebted to the advice of the following people who kindly shared their insights and experiences with us during the researching and writing of this book. We greatly appreciate their help. However, any errors or omissions are entirely down to the authors themselves.

Many thanks to:

Sheila Bates, Human Resources Manager, KPN Orange Belgium; Andrea Burrows, Managing Director, Associates in Advertising; Cary Cooper, BUPA professor of organisational psychology and health, UMIST; Joan Coulter, Consultant, Beament Leslie Thomas; Hamish Davidson, Partner and Head of the UK Executive Search & Selection Division, PricewaterhouseCoopers; Alan Dickinson, Chief Executive, Jobsfinancial.com; Mike Dodd, Managing Director, Academy HR Services Group; Richard Donkin, columnist for The Financial Times; Jonathan R. Ebsworth, Partner, Reid Minty, Solicitors; Dr Clive Fletcher, Managing Director of Personnel Assessment Ltd, and formerly Professor of Occupational Psychology at Goldsmiths' College, University of London; Ian Harvey, Independent Executive Search Consultant; Linda Holbeche, Director of Research, Roffey Park; Simon Howard, Sunday Times Jobfile columnist; Elaine Howe, Co-founder of Working Options; Gary Hoyte, Director, Gary Hoyte Consulting Ltd (HR Consultants) and formerly HR Director of Scope; Dr Gareth Jones, Managing Partner of organisational consulting firm Creative Management Associates, Visiting Professor at INSEAD, and formerly Director of HR and Internal Communications at the BBC; Brendan Keelan, Partner Howgate Sable (Executive Search & Selection Consultants); Bob Leach, Director, Resources Connection; Chris Long, Partner in senior executive search consultancy Whitehead Mann; Shana Mazin, Media Consultant, AIA; Terry Nolan, Senior Management Development Manager, Unilever; Robert Peasnell, UK Managing Director, McCann-Erickson Recruitment; Graham Perkins, HR Consultant & Freelance Career Counsellor (Formerly Manager, Executive Search & Selection Division, Deloitte & Touche); Stewart Rogers, Managing Director, The Rogers Partnership Ltd; Sesh Sukhdeo, Vice President – Europe, Qwiz; Chris Tanner, Company Director & Independent Business Consultant (formerly Director of Training at Deloitte & Touche); Mike Walmsley, Managing Director, Pro-active Consulting; Kay Wesley, Vice President of Corporate Operations and Strategy, TopJobs ; Suzzane Wood, Partner & Head of Financial Management Practice, Odgers Ray & Berndtson (Executive Search Consultants).

Part I

The Strategic Environment

Chapter 1

The Business Agenda

Successful businesses thrive by means of their ability to adapt and innovate. Those businesses – in which we include public companies accountable to demanding shareholders, privately owned businesses and public sector bodies trying to meet public expectations – need talented people to do so. How you tap into that talent, through what relationships and for how long, is subject to on-going change.

Talent is the key

Businesses need people. Not just any people, but talented people. Microchips, machines or raw materials cannot innovate. It is people who have to come up with the vision and the ideas to move organisations forward.

Of course, talent means different things to different organisations, as management consultant Michael Williams, writing in the magazine *People Management*, points out. Nevertheless, all organisations need it in some form. Williams offers the following definition of a talented person as being 'someone who regularly demonstrates exceptional ability and achievement either over a range of activities, or within a specialised field of expertise'.[1]

Can you do without that? Not if you want to succeed in your sector. An organisation that wants to be a leader must attract, motivate and retain the most able people in their field – be they designers, marketeers or chief executives, brain surgeons, human genome researchers or hospital managers.

Research by management consultancy McKinsey & Co has provided firm evidence of the difference quality people can make. Companies with the best talent-management practices (scoring in the top quintile) outperform their industry's mean return to shareholders by 22%. The consultants also found that, in one manufacturing company, the best plant managers actually increased profits by 130%.[2]

The war for talent

Competition for the most able people is tough: hence the 'war for talent' descriptor increasingly used in recent years to emphasise the tough time that organisations have been facing in their attempts to recruit top-class people.

Frontline reports

Does the war for talent really exist? Yes. Dr Gareth Jones, formerly Director of HR and Internal Communications at the BBC and currently Visiting Professor at INSEAD, has no doubt that organisations face a key challenge in recruiting the people who really make a difference. He says: 'There certainly is a war for talent. It's not about finding good people – finding good people is OK. It's finding people who can transform your organisation. That's what's hard.'

Terry Nolan, Senior Management Development Manager at Unilever, agrees: 'Where it really hits you is when you want to get people for jobs which combine high levels of technical or professional expertise with high levels of leadership skills. There are a lot of good technical experts around, but there are very few people who manage to combine those with real leadership quality. It's the leading of people, the building of visions, the building of teams, allied to having the drive for implementation – that's what's hard to find.'

Moreover, star players need to be able to adapt to changing times, Nolan explains: 'This is where the war for talent really starts to hit you, because you need people with behavioural awareness and flexibility. You want the gold nuggets – the people who can adapt their organisational behaviour, but who don't lose their authenticity. These people are very rare and that's why it's called the "war for talent".'

As Nolan explains, the top talent shortage is not limited by region: 'The war for talent is just as fierce in China as it is in

Europe. Companies will pay top dollar for young, well-educated local people in emerging market economies. The competition is ferocious.'

Frontline research

Management consultancy McKinsey & Co initially investigated the challenges facing businesses in recruiting top talent in its 1997 survey, *The War for Talent*. It revisited the topic again in 2000 and found that the situation had become even tougher. This later research surveyed 6,900 managers at 56 large and medium-sized US companies; it found that 89% thought it more difficult to attract talented people in 2000 than it had been three years before, while 90% thought it more difficult to retain them. A mere 7% strongly agreed that their companies had enough talented managers in order to pursue all or most of the promising business opportunities they identified. Only 14% of the managers in McKinsey's 2000 survey (an actual fall on the 23% recorded in 1997) strongly agreed that their companies actually attracted highly talented people.[3]

The follow-up 2000 research undeniably verified McKinsey's earlier predictions: 'Companies are about to be engaged in a war for senior executive talent that will remain a defining characteristic of their competitive landscape for decades to come. Yet most are ill prepared, and even the best are vulnerable.'[4]

The McKinsey findings also indicated some of the reasons for this talent shortage: the shrinking pool of 35–40 year olds in the US, and in most developed nations; meanwhile more of the best qualified people were opting to work for start-ups and small businesses rather than large, traditional employers.[5]

In addition, employees have become more willing to take control of their careers and move around between employers. Individuals increasingly make active choices about the kinds of organisations they want to work for, the challenges and opportunities they desire and the rewards they require.

In his book, *Winning the Talent Wars*, Bruce Tulgan says: 'This is the essence of the talent wars: In the new economy, every term of employment – schedules, location, assignments, coworkers, pay, and more – will be open to negotiation, whether you like

it or not. The most valuable talent will have the most negotiating power. Every employment relationship will last exactly
as long as the terms are agreeable to all the parties.'[6]

New-style relationships

One of the reasons that recruitment has become so important
is that organisations these days have to do a lot of it. Once upon
a time people entering the workforce could reasonably expect
to spend the majority of their working lives with a single
employer. Now we have entered an era of short-term employment relationships.

A paternalistic past

Even up until the late 1980s or early 1990s it was still widely
accepted that, as long as employees worked hard and kept
their noses clean, their employers would look after them – they
could have a job for life. The unspoken psychological contract
between employer and employee was a relatively simple one:
loyal employees worked hard and were rewarded by steady
progression up through the multiple managerial levels. The
most able could eventually expect to make it to the top within
the same organisation they had joined at the start of their
career. Employers looked after their employees' careers, keeping a paternalistic eye on their development and rewards.

Recruitment advertising in this era reflected the lifetime of service concept. Take Shell. Back in 1980 the company's sales pitch
to candidates played heavily on the fact that, by sticking around
and doing their bit for the company, new recruits would one
day be rewarded with a job in the upper reaches of the hierarchy. Recruitment brochures would typically picture someone middle aged, sitting behind a desk, pen in hand. 'Meet
Brian', the text would say. 'Brian joined our internal audit
department in 1962, where he spent several years coming into
close contact with most business units.' Brian's career would
then be summarised, detailing a series of backroom, unglam-
orous jobs, a few years in an overseas subsidiary and then
his eventual breakthrough into a more high profile, strategic
management role back at head office. Brian clearly had a good

job now, but it had taken him almost 30 years to get there. 'Come and join us and enjoy the same success as Brian' would be the brochure's final punch line.

Shell was not alone. All big companies based their recruitment drives on promises for the future. Join now, work hard, and leave on a high in 30–40 years' time. Employees appreciated the implied job security and were prepared to put up with some drudgery relatively early on in their careers. As long as they got there in the end, slow progress was okay.

Tougher times

Then came the recession. Suddenly employees were being laid off as businesses were forced to make incisive cuts in over-heads. Coincidentally, business theory had been developing in new ways with the emergence of the concept of re-engi-neering. Michael Hammer, a former Computer Science Pro-fessor at MIT, used the term initially in the late 1980s with reference to the impact technology could have on business processes. It became associated, however, with the wholesale redesign of organisational structures. In his book, *Blood, Sweat and Tears*, *Financial Times* columnist Richard Donkin describes re-engineering as 'paring away the flesh of com-panies down to the pure white bones of profit'. Along with re-engineering came delayering, downsizing and outsourcing. Jobs that had once been secure and respected were ruthlessly cut away.

The new environment caused major shockwaves, as Donkin explains: 'Layoffs had been a harsh fact of life for many in man-ual employment, alleviated briefly among those born into that generation of steady economic growth after World War II. But layoffs among white-collar management were almost unheard of until the axe began to fall in the late 1980s and early 1990s. It fell in the service sector, perhaps more heavily than it did in manufacturing. It cut a swathe through the middle of large corporations, taking with it middle-class, middle-aged, middle management. Arthur Miller's version of white-collar obsoles-cence had come home to roost, as thousands of managers contemplated Willy Loman's nightmare of rejection in *Death of a Salesman*.'[7]

We consider the dramatic impact such job losses have had on the employee mindset in Chapter 2: The Candidate Agenda. However, as far as employers were concerned, a new era had begun. There were no longer jobs for life. New management theories could radically change the shape and nature of business life. What was required was a staffing philosophy that ensured organisations had the skills required where and when they required them.

The new era

This new corporate attitude to employment has had repercussions in several ways. First, as described above, jobs for life are no longer part of the employer's side of the psychological contract. If there is a real, productive job to be done, all well and good. But employers now make no bones about that fact that, as management practices, processes, markets and technology change, so that job may disappear.

Secondly, jobs that were automatically considered permanent may now be seen as temporary. Before the 1990s it was common for employers to ask recruitment consultants to find them permanent recruits, even if the immediate skills need was recognised as a temporary one. 'We need someone to come and manage this subsidiary for nine months,' the client would say. 'But we'll find them something else to do when that's over.' The approach in part reflected the employer's presumption that there was only one kind of worker who really counted: a full-time, permanent one. Temporary or part-time staff were not taken seriously.

All that has changed, again encouraged by the new focus on organisational efficiency that came with re-engineering. If there is an identified skill need for nine months, why commit the organisation to paying for that skill for any longer than that? Interim management and temporary work in general have therefore grown in favour.

Flexible access to talent

In this new world of employment, organisations have to recognise that business performance is driven by the skills and talent to which an organisation has access. These skills may come from traditional full-time workers, as well as from other non-traditional employment sources.

The esteemed Charles Handy commented on the change and predicted the new world order in his book *The Age of Unreason*. There he set out the concept of the 'Shamrock Organisation', which has three integrated leaves: the central core, the contractual fringe and the ancillary workforce. In Handy's vision, the central core would contain the essential managers, professionals and technicians who help to maintain the organisation's culture, knowledge and direction. The second leaf – the contractual fringe – would take account of the non-essential contractual work that did not need to be retained in-house. Finally, the ancillary workforce would be made up of temporary and part-time workers, whose highly flexible status would enable the organisation to react quickly to fluctuating skill and service needs. In the shamrock, the three parts form one leaf; so a shamrock organisation would be a corporate whole formed from a flexible, tripartite structure.[8]

The changing nature of the workforce exceeded even respected pundits' predictions. At the start of the 1980s Charles Handy forecast that by the year 2000 less than half of the British working population would be in conventional full-time jobs on indefinite contracts. Looking back on that forecast in his book *The Elephant and the Flea*, Handy describes the prophecy as 'foolhardy'. However, as he notes, he was proved too conservative in his estimate. 'As it turned out, by the year 2000 the proportion of the British labour force on those indefinite period contracts in full-time employment had fallen to 40 per cent ...'.[9]

Management guru Tom Peters has also noted the shifting workforce patterns. He has predicted that in the 21st century only one-third of jobs will be permanent, while the rest will be temporary, contract-based, part-time or teleworking roles.

The rise of the joint venture

We see the new relationship between employer and employee developing as a joint venture. In this venture, employers recognise that the talent and skills people have to offer sit at the heart of a successful business. However, the demand that employers will have for these skills will change; organisations need the flexibility to shape their future directions so as to best meet the demands of shareholders and other stakeholders.

Therefore, the new relationship means that the employer guarantees no particular length of employment contract. However, the employer recognises an obligation to help employees maintain their skills, which itself benefits the employer, but also reassures the employee that their marketability is being maintained. If the employer can no longer continue to offer them a job, they have some reassurance that they will be attractive to other employers in the market. Employers must therefore offer training and development and do their best to provide employees with new challenges in the workplace.

Charles Handy in *The Hungry Spirit* comments on the change, saying: 'it is clear that the psychological contract between employers and employed has changed. The smart jargon now talks of guaranteeing "employability" not "employment", which, being interpreted, means don't count on us, count on yourself, but we'll try to help if we can.'[10]

This does not mean that employers cannot be creative in the psychological contracts they develop, or that there is any one way of creating a joint venture with their employees. Dr Gareth Jones advises employers to be honest and realistic in developing their own versions: 'You have to be honest about your psychological contract, but design it around what is critical for your business. Take a pharmaceutical business. If you are recruiting leading edge scientists to work in R&D, they are not interested in whether there is a car park; they want to know whether you will fund their research obsessions.'

As for employees, they no longer anticipate spending the majority of their working lives with one employer. Instead a typical career is expected to involve a series of job moves between different organisations. The factors which shape a career and the frequency of moves may vary from individual to individual, but will include issues such as general job satisfaction, the extent of new challenges, opportunities for skills development as well as financial rewards.

There is, as Bruce Tulgan notes, a free market for talent. In *Winning the Talent Wars*, Tulgan writes: 'The talent wars ... are growing out of a fundamental paradigm shift in the employer–employee relationship: from the old, slow-moving, rigid, pay-your-dues-and-climb-the-ladder model to the new fast-moving, increasingly efficient free market for talent.'[11]

Recruitment: the heart of business success

The McKinsey consultants identified a number of recommended steps that organisations should take to try to win the war for talent.[12] These included:

- making talent management a burning priority (for example, setting performance standards and making line managers accountable for the talent of their team);
- creating a winning employee value proposition (which provides a compelling answer to the question, 'Why would I want to work here?'). This is linked to creating an appealing employer brand, a challenge we consider in Chapter 3: Strategies for Successful Recruitment;
- sourcing great talent (which forms the core focus of this book);
- developing talent aggressively (providing challenges, giving feedback, trying harder to retain high performers, and dealing with poor performers). We consider some of these issues in Chapter 17: Re-recruitment and Chapter 18: Firing.

Recruiting Excellence focuses primarily on the challenge of sourcing great talent. We believe that successful recruitment lies at the heart of business success.

What is the business agenda in terms of recruitment? Put simply, it is to gain access to the best talent, when and where your organisation needs it, for as long as it needs that talent.

Recruitment plays a key role in winning the talent wars, and not just in making sure that fresh, appropriate talent is being introduced into the organisation. Yes, recruitment involves attracting and selecting appropriate people, but it also involves setting the expectations of those new recruits; on day one you want to make sure that hot-shot Phil is inspired, rather than let down.

Recruitment also involves identifying from the start of the employment relationship the kinds of challenges that the incoming individual is looking for and the kinds of development that may be required to keep that talent growing. Recruitment has to be aligned with the overall training and development activities of the HR function.

Business strategists are also now talking about re-recruitment. Recruitment cannot be considered a one-off function that is finished once the chosen candidate walks through the office doors on her first day of work. Every day those people identified as having the skills the organisation needs must be re-recruited. This has to be done by a continual reaffirmation of the values and challenges offered by the role.

How an organisation approaches its recruitment process, and the effort it puts into doing it excellently, has huge implications for its success for years ahead.

A word on recession

When the idea for this book was first conceived, although the dot.com bubble had already burst there was still widespread confidence about the strength of the global economy. The tragic events in New York on 11 September 2001 were yet to come. Since then, concern over a global slowdown and UK downturn has grown, although predictions of how tough things could get remain mixed.

So what impact might an economic downturn have on the war for talent? There has been no shortage of reports of mass redundancies. Does this mean there will be a period of talent glut? Will power swing back to recruiting organisations, enabling them to pick and choose? Will employees be more fearful of unemployment than in the past, and so be willing to stay in an unsatisfactory position where before they would have swiftly moved on?

Some of these repercussions may happen, to some extent. Uncertainty over the global economy may deter people from moving, worried that they may suffer from 'last in, first out' syndrome if their new employer has to make redundancies.

However, employers cannot expect things to be easy. We suggest that the war for talent will not come to a sudden end.

The best quality personnel will remain in demand. As most honest business people admit, almost any fool can make money in a boom time; it is when times get tough that real talent stands out. The skills needed to be successful may change slightly, of course; those skilled in making cost-saving efficiencies may find themselves more feted than those whose gung-ho approach, although valuable in optimistic, expansive times, may be too costly in the short-term.

So, employers cannot expect that the quality people will automatically stick with them or will be banging on their doors for work. They will still need as much wooing as before.

Effective wooing depends on an understanding of what the modern employee looks for in an employer and a career. Without this knowledge, how can you hope to attract, motivate and retain the talented people you need? We consider the motivations of the modern employee in the next chapter, The Candidate Agenda.

Chapter 2

The Candidate Agenda

If employers have changed their view of their relationships with employees, so those employees have changed their expectations of their employers.

As we noted in the previous chapter, employees no longer anticipate spending the majority of their working lives with a single organisation. When employers began cutting out huge wedges from the management hierarchy in the early 1990s, so employees realised that they no longer needed, or were expected, to show loyalty to an employer; the umbilical cord of trust between employer and employee had suddenly been broken.

Swedish academics Kjell Nordström and Jodas Ridderstråle see the potential excitement in this new world order. In their book *Funky Business* the self-proclaimed 'funksters', clearly two men who enjoy their work, explain that 'the job' is dead. 'Throughout most of the twentieth century, managers averaged one job and one career. Now, we are talking about two careers and seven jobs. The days of the long-serving corporate man, safe and sound in the dusty recesses of the corporation, are long gone. Soon the emphasis will be on getting a life instead of a career, and work will be viewed as a series of gigs or projects.'[1]

The rise of the career mercenary

In today's world, employees are increasingly acting as independent agents, moving from employer to employer in search of more challenging work, better development opportunities, access to leading-edge technology or improved financial rewards.

In *Kickstart Your Career*, our job-hunter's guide to building successful careers in this new working environment, we described the modern worker as a 'career mercenary'. We explained: 'In our definition, career mercenaries are independent agents who make positive employment choices, moving from one organisation to another, depending on the opportunities and the rewards available. They remain loyal to themselves, placing their employment needs as their top priority, although they provide their current employer with the best possible service they can, so that both employer and employee benefit from the new flexibility. The employer becomes, in a sense, the employee's client.'[2]

Other writers have described the modern worker in similar ways. In *Winning the Talent Wars*, Bruce Tulgan describes the 'rising tide of the free-agent mind-set among individuals in direct response to employers' disavowal of job security'. Tulgan says: 'Individuals have taken responsibility for their own careers, and now most are looking out for themselves first and foremost in their relationships with employers.'[3]

One word of warning. We are not arguing that all employees want the same things. When we first considered writing about the career mercenary, a few friends and colleagues expressed concern about the term. Surely, some people do still seek a long-term role, they said.

Absolutely. But we believe that achieving a long-term relationship with an employer is not incompatible with a career mercenary outlook. Descriptions such as the 'career mercenary' or 'free agent' do not mean that all employees will necessarily want to move between numerous employers; they simply highlight the potential for such mobility. There will, of course, always be some people who satisfy their needs within a single, permanent long-term employment contract, if only because the maintenance of a long-term relationship is particularly important to them.

The fall of the wage slave

Looking back to our parents' generation, it seems that people in a sense were grateful for the work they could get. If you found salaried employment with a steady career path, why rock the boat and look elsewhere?

These days we are far less willing to take what we have got and assume that is the best there is. Wage slaves are fewer and farther between. But why is this?

A number of reasons present themselves:

- acceptance of and desire for job mobility;
- increasing numbers of cash rich, time poor people;
- employees' greater knowledge of their potential value.

Job mobility

As individual employees, we are generally more prepared to move around. Few of us now believe that we have a safe job where we are for life. Things change, markets collapse, and consumer trends come and go. So, there is less to be lost by moving from one employer to another. In fact, in many ways there is much to be gained – other employers will value experienced gained from a range of situations.

A survey carried out by Robert Half International on behalf of *Management Today* found that over half of those aged under 35 had already worked at four or more companies. Furthermore, 73% of this age group said they wanted to move on from their current employer, while almost the same percentage (72%) of the 55-plus age group wanted to stay where they were. Two-thirds (67%) of all respondents and 77% of under 35s ranked the job for life bottom of a list of key demands for their working lives.

So, what motivated the younger age group to change jobs? Almost a third (32%) said the desire to gain more responsibility would have the greatest influence on their decision to change jobs, while another 18% cited finding a greater challenge and just 14% said pay alone would motivate them. Across all age groups, respondents agreed that job satisfaction was key to their working lives.[4]

Cash rich, time poor

Towards the end of the 1990s the phrase 'downsizing' became a familiar term for people who had decided they had sacrificed enough time and energy in demanding jobs and who were now prepared to change jobs and take less money in return for a more relaxed lifestyle.

Many people in their 30s and 40s have higher standards of living than ever before, and have achieved these levels more quickly than their parents could have dreamed possible. With economic power comes economic choice. City analysts who have sacrificed personal time to work long hours in return for big pay packets find that the incremental value of further bonuses decreases rapidly after 10 or 15 years; time becomes the valuable commodity. They are rich in wealth and poor in time, and unless their employers can find a way to give them more time, many will head off in search of a different lifestyle.

Research findings released by careers consultancy Penna Sanders and Sidney in September 2001, based on information from over 1000 companies in 24 countries, found that seven out of 10 women and a third of men would sacrifice income for more time. However, a third of businesses have no flexible working policy at all. Comparing geographical trends, the most people-centred businesses, providing employees with the most liberal policies on working hours, telecommuting and the best work–life balance, were found primarily in the USA and Scandinavia.

Value awareness

Most people now have a greater awareness of their worth. Salary surveys and news stories on the job market and career movers are far more common than they were 10 years ago. People increasingly know what they could be worth if they moved to a more successful or dynamic organisation.

Even moving itself generates a pay rise. Pay structures, for example, no longer reward loyalty. Research over the last few years has shown that employees who stay with their employer could generally expect an annual pay rise of around 3–4%, an amount just ahead of inflation. In contrast, people who change jobs enjoy an average pay rise of around 9%.

The dot.com factor

There is no doubting that the dramatic growth of the dot.com sector, the somewhat feverish rush to set up, invest and work in Internet-based companies, has had an effect on the recruitment marketplace and the expectations of individual workers. It was not just the huge potential financial rewards that made people check out of respectable blue-chip jobs and check-in to a small, uncertain dot.com office. It was also the buzz, the casting off of old assumptions about how you do things, the potential to create new business models.

The fact that you probably did not have to wear a suit and tie (or the female equivalent) was just a by-product of the dot.com office culture. Interestingly, it is also one that many blue chips decided to introduce themselves, although not always in a way well-received by their current employees who had invested in smart suits and now had to work out what 'smart casual' really meant.

Dot.coms offered much more than a disregard for having to dress in the corporate uniform. The culture was seen as dynamic, entrepreneurial, creative, youthful, perhaps even anarchic, certainly more democratic, with small teams sharing in anticipated share option gains. On top of this dot.coms offered the chance to be in the vanguard of a new way of doing business, of providing services, of working and living.

The fact that so many dot.coms went belly up provided a bit of a reality check. The virtues of established blue chips were highlighted, putting a bit more balance into the employment marketplace.

But even experience of failure is good experience. People who emerged from collapsed Internet ventures could sell themselves to new employers on the grounds that they knew what *not* to do, the warning signs, the hitches and glitches. They had been bloodied in the battle and emerged better armed for the next e-based skirmish.

Generation X

The dot.com phenomenon highlighted how quickly established business practices and assumptions can change. Such change is likely to happen most rapidly and most dramatically amongst the younger generations, the traditional challengers of the status quo.

Employers have increasingly recognised that many younger people entering the workforce have strikingly different outlooks and aspirations. The term 'Generation X' was coined to sum up this new population group, people comfortable with technology and a fast-moving world.

In 1998, Robert Half combined with McCann-Erickson to research the aspirations of mid-20s accountants by holding a series of forums. The aim was to find out what the career hot buttons of these Generation X-ers were, what organisations they respected and would consider working for, what drove their career ambitions. As a cross-section of young professionals, their opinions suggest the factors that all employers need to bear in mind if they want to attract the motivated and skilled leaders of the future.

Brand value

One striking finding was that a number of companies kept emerging as favoured employers, with Virgin Group by far the most popular. The reasons given focused on the perceived culture there. 'The culture and environment are different' said one participant. Of course, the people surveyed could not know this for certain because they had not worked there. What these respondents were doing was making assumptions about the culture and environment based on the brand image that Virgin has created. Other organisations repeatedly favoured by the focus groups were Mars, the BBC, Nestlé and Andersen Consulting (now Accenture), again all organisations with strong brand images.

Short-term aspirations

In terms of career aspirations, our sample group thought that it was acceptable to move on to a new employer relatively quickly; the acceptable timescales given ranged between 18 months and two and a quarter years after joining. This group were certainly not thinking about long-term career options with one employer. Asked whether their previous employers could have done anything to stop them leaving, the answer was a resounding 'No'.

They were certainly career option browsers; almost 70% said they regularly looked through job advertisements. They also expected to achieve a salary uplift when they did move, saying they would not move to a job offering the same remuneration. They said they were attracted by advertisements with large salaries, that had a large, bright format and that promoted an interesting role.

Younger workers also expect rapid results. If those results are not forthcoming, employees will take their talent elsewhere. Research for Unilever in the 1990s, based on conversations with leavers, tried to establish why some employees were leaving after only a few years with the company. Why were not these people following the traditional path of slow and steady progression?

The consistent message generated by the research was that talented leavers saw Unilever as a 'slow moving escalator'. These people recognised that there were career opportunities, but that these were slow in coming. They were not prepared to do their time and wait until the escalator reached the top; they wanted to make career leaps, to experience new challenges and rewards far more quickly than they felt was possible if they stayed where they were.

Generation Y

According to *People Management* magazine, the term Generation Y was coined by Eric Chester (a motivational speaker in the USA and also an expert on Generation X) to describe people born between 1977 and 1994. These youngsters view laptops and cellphones, AIDS and crack cocaine as unsurprising aspects of life. Chester characterises this group as adaptable, innovative and unthreatened by technology, resilient, talented and committed, but also impatient, disrespectful, image-driven, blunt and sceptical. Recruiting and retaining such people requires employers to be honest, lead by example and understand where Generation Y is coming from.[5]

New graduates clearly fall into the Generation Y catchment area. Recent research conducted by research and management consulting firm Universum Communications looked at the career thoughts of 5726 final-year undergraduates in 43 UK universities. According to the Universum Graduate Survey, the UK graduates' ideal employer is the Foreign and Common-wealth Office, followed by … Virgin Group (which took second place the preceding two years as well) and Accenture.[6] There is therefore a striking similarity to the Robert Half/McCann-Erickson findings for Generation X preferences.

Universum's results also show that, in general, graduates have a liking for technology-based companies. IBM, Vodafone, Marconi and WS Atkins all rose up the rankings while Cisco Systems and Sun Microsystems were new entrants.

Work–life balance

Commenting on the Universum Graduate Survey, *Guardian* writer Ian Wylie noted that it revealed 'an ambitious, self-confident, and risk-taking generation'. However, these graduates were not just after big bucks, as Wylie noted: '...their vision of their future also includes a healthy balance between their career and their life outside of work. A high proportion are keen to work overseas, yet a quarter are also keen to choose an industry and an employer which enables them to make a contribution to society.'[7]

Interestingly, only 30% of survey respondents cited building a sound financial base as a career goal. And the vast majority were not anticipating burning too many late night hours at work. A massive 78% expected to work no more than 45 hours a week in their first job.

Universum's conclusion was that this year's crop of graduates were less interested in 'what's in it for me?' but more turned on by work–life balance and personal development issues. They wanted the opportunity to develop sound skills and gain respected experience in organisations with a good brand name.

This research confirms the findings of other similar studies. For example, in a survey of 2500 students in 11 countries by PricewaterhouseCoopers, 57% of respondents said balancing work and their personal life was their primary career goal.

Both surveys were conducted before the economic downturn and US tragedy in September 2001, when everyone's mood – that of graduates and employers – was more bullish. However, had the survey been conducted later the likelihood is that its findings would only have been emphasised. In tougher times, past evidence shows that people focus even more on issues such as personal development, job interest and work–life balance, leaving their money-oriented focus to times when things are booming.

Across all generations, demand for new ways of working is growing. The Management Agenda 2001, a study by executive education and research organisation Roffey Park, found that 60% of middle and senior managers surveyed thought there was a culture of presenteeism within their organisation; 86% worked longer hours than their contracted working week, with 19% working 15 hours extra a week on average. Although a small majority (53%) said they were satisfied with the balance between their work and personal lives, of the significant minority who were not, 38% said they were considering leaving their current employer specifically to get a better balance.

Individuals increasingly want flexibility to be able to work part-time, flexitime or to work from home (at least occasionally). Employers who support such policies, who appreciate the importance of work–life balance issues to today's workforce, can improve their success rates in both attracting and retaining talented people. We revisit this issue in Chapter 17: Re-recruitment.

Employer-specific research

Employers who want to be successful recruiters must understand what their potential employees are looking for from their working lives. The only way to attract people is to understand their needs and desires and react accordingly. While general trends can be understood from broad-brush surveys, the dynamics affecting an individual employer in a specific industry can vary.

However, despite the fact that a top performer can make a huge difference to the success of the organisation, few employers invest time and money in researching the attitudes and expectations of potential members of their workforce. This is despite the fact that the same organisations will spend millions researching the preferences of their customers. We suggest that the same attention, and financial commitment, could usefully be given to investigating what it is that talented employees are looking for.

Employers who take their recruitment and talent management seriously recognise that they need to understand the aspirations and frustrations of their current, future and past employees. Unilever is one company that has understood this concept. When the company developed its business strategy based on faster growth, it recognised that it needed to increase its recruitment rate for top, talented executives. In order to do this, Unilever recognised that it needed to understand better why people joined, why people stayed and why people left the company. This information has been used to develop the company's employer brand, a topic we revisit in Chapter 3: Strategies for Successful Recruitment. For Unilever, the findings were key to understanding how the company could go forward in improving its attractiveness, improving its retention and providing the talent engine for the growth it desired.

Other companies too are increasingly making efforts to understand the motivations of employees. One international group decided to survey its young European managers – aged 35 or under – to try to identify the key factors that impacted on an individual's decision to leave or to stay. The research identified these to be as follows:

1. pace of career development;
2. salary/compensation/remuneration;
3. challenges;
4. international exposure;
5. leadership and responsibility;
6. other offers/opportunities;
7. job satisfaction;
8. personal development/growth;
9. quality of leadership/vision/strategy;
10. job security.

The company also investigated the reasons why trainees decided to join it in the first place. It found that trainees across Europe joined the company for three key reasons:

- they liked the people they met at interview;
- they perceived the group not to be a threatening organisation, but instead, one with a supportive and team-working culture;
- they believed it had a respected training programme.

This kind of information is worth its weight in gold to an employer who wants to maximise its appeal to job candidates.

The joint venture

Employees are increasingly willing to see the relationship they have with their employers as a joint venture. They are increasingly saying: 'We'll work for you, provide our best skills and talent, but we expect to share in the added value we deliver (through share options, bonuses or whatever). We will keep our skills up to date, but you must help us do this by providing effective training and giving us the time to focus on it. However, we won't guarantee to stay with you long term. We will be looking at the job market and will be prepared to move on if we believe our career options will be better elsewhere.'

Understanding this attitude can help employers to attract and retain people in mutually beneficial ways. As an employer your recruitment focus should be on enabling a mutually well-informed decision about whether you and the candidate have something to offer each other and whether the two of you will be better off by joining forces. That is the attitude that you need to shape your recruitment processes and culture.

There is also a need for flexibility in recruitment style and strategy. As we have considered above, younger generations do not necessarily see things the same way as those who have gone before them. We have no doubt that career mercenaries at different stages in their careers may want different things. A young graduate beginning a first job after university may pay more attention to training schemes than an employee of 45 with an increased interest in employer pension contributions.

Employers who want to tap into the talent in all age groups need to be able to respond to the needs of each of them; there is no 'one size fits all' solution to the challenge of recruiting excellence. Employers need to be able to segment their workforce and their targeted recruits. A mid-20s member of Generation X may be more likely to move on after two years than an employee in his late 40s who places a higher premium on job continuity.

Employers need to develop recruitment strategies that complement the new joint venture they have with their employees, and that reflect the importance of understanding the needs of different employee groups. We now move on to look at the kinds of recruitment strategies that may be needed to reconcile the business and candidate agenda.

Chapter 3

Strategies for Successful Recruitment

Employers are competing in a war for talent. They need effective recruitment strategies to maximise their chances of success.

Recruitment can itself be broken down into two key constituent factors: attraction and selection. First of all, potential applicants have to be attracted to the organisation in order to apply for a vacancy. Then the recruiter has to select the applicants who appear most likely to meet the needs of the role in question, and who are most closely aligned with the organisation's culture and values. Finally, employers also need to develop a real recruitment culture that places the highest priority on drawing talent into the organisation.

Playing the attraction game

It goes without saying that the more attractive the recruiting organisation, the more likely potential employees are to apply to work there. The most attractive employers will not even need to advertise to receive job applications.

Companies with candidate appeal receive thousands, hundreds of thousands, of speculative applications from keen applicants every year. These tend to be high profile, blue-chip companies with strong brand images that individuals want to be associated with.

Take British Airways. The UK's flagship airline has at times received around 80,000 applications a year. The weight of applicant interest meant that several full-time staff were employed solely to handle these applications. Marks & Spencer, although it has had a fairly rough ride recently, for a long time had extremely high candidate appeal.

On the one hand, such a level of interest creates a huge administrative burden on the internal recruitment team. However, this is a sign of the organisation's success in creating candidate appeal. Companies who receive thousands of applications are winning the attraction game.

In practical terms the attraction game has to apply to every detail of the recruitment process. For example, you need to ensure that the personalities candidates meet are the personalities you want them to associate with your organisation. As we consider in Chapter 11: Interviewing: Technique Tips, the people you put forward as interviewers will have a major impact on interviewees; the candidates will take the interviewer's characteristics and transpose them onto the organisation. So if the interviewer appears intolerant and untalented, that is how the organisation will seem to the candidate. Would you join it?

Knowledge is power

Employers need to understand what they have to offer candidates if they want to be successful recruiters and maximise their employer brand impact. Robert Half International was once appointed to help one of the leading accountancy firms recruit around 60 new consultants. The firm wanted to attract people from industry, who had trained in management accounting and reinforced their qualification with some solid business experience.

The recruiters wanted to get an advertising campaign out fast. The Robert Half team said, 'OK, but first we need to know what your sales proposition is. Why would your target candidates want to come and work for you?'

We thought this was an important question because after all, the target applicants were people who had opted to gain their financial qualifications in industry, rather than in a professional practice. So why would they want to change cultures now?

Surprisingly, the firm could not tell us. So how were they expecting to create a coherent sales message to attract people before they could even begin selecting them?

You have to know what you have to offer before you can hope to recruit successfully. If you do not know, you need to do some research:

- ask new joiners why they joined;
- ask people who stay why they stay;
- ask people who leave why they leave;
- seek feedback on external perceptions of the organisation.

Ignorance is certainly not bliss in recruitment.

Employer branding

Organisations have begun to formalise their need for candidate appeal, and increasingly talk about the importance of creating an employer brand.

Engaging Employees through Your Brand, a report by management research organisation The Conference Board, uses the following definition: 'The employer brand establishes the identity of the firm as an employer. It encompasses the firm's values, systems, policies, and behaviours toward the objectives of attracting, motivating, and retaining the firm's current and potential employees.'[1]

Dr Gareth Jones, formerly Director of HR and Internal Communications at the BBC, and currently Managing Partner of Organisational Consulting Firm Creative Management Associates, says that employer branding should not be seen in too narrow a sense. 'You are trying to say how the organisation feels. Employer branding isn't just about the employment relationship narrowly defined; it's not just saying, "We are good employers; we are fully compliant with equal opportunities legislation." It's about how it will feel to work there. Are you the kind of person who will fit in at Electronic Arts Inc, or would you be happier in the Foreign Office? So employer branding is about conveying the character of the organisation, its personality. The brand is the outward manifestation of culture; you can't be what you aren't.'

The Conference Board's report was based on surveys with executives responsible for corporate or employer branding, or both, in 137 companies. These executives saw the top goals of the employer brand as being to recruit employees, retain employees, achieve a reputation as an employer of choice as well as to help existing employees internalise the company's values. The report found that 'a lack of employer brand identity can be an obstacle to successful hiring strategies in tight talent markets'.[2]

Although the employer brand is distinct from the organisation's corporate brand, it is closely related to it, since the corporate brand also embodies company values and culture. A strong corporate brand itself plays a vital role in establishing an organisation's status as an employer of choice.

Employer branding activity therefore becomes particularly important where an organisation does not itself have a strong corporate brand. For example, businesses that transact with other businesses, rather than end-user customers, can find it particularly difficult to create a strong public brand awareness.

The Conference Board's report sought to identify factors which determined why some employer brands were more successful than others. It found that effective employer brands were:

- holistic – applying throughout the company and throughout internal and external markets;
- known and understood throughout the company;
- known in the employment marketplace.

Ineffective branding ideas were identified as those that simply said: 'We are a great place to work' but didn't actually differentiate the company from competitors, or those that simply rehashed the company's mission statement. Brands that emerged simply as a response to competitors creating an employer brand, or where the brand was created by consultants and 'parachuted' into employees, were also seen as less likely to succeed. In addition, employer brands that remained a separate effort, with a different message, from the marketing brand were also seen as ineffective, since the one could not reinforce the other.[3]

Robert Peasnell, UK Managing Director of Advertising Business McCann-Erickson Recruitment, says that although clients frequently talk about employer branding and are aware of the concept, few understand it properly. He says: 'A lot think about it at the more superficial end, for example, linking it to product advertising. However, employer branding in the fullest sense is about effectively managing the employment experience of your people – that's potential staff and existing ones. Therefore it has implications for the whole employment experience – how you structure your remuneration packages, how you deal with maternity and paternity leave, your culture, how effectively you communicate within the organisation. It's not just about the front-end, glossy marketing bit.'

When KPN Orange the mobile telecommunications company was setting up in Belgium, it faced a tough recruitment challenge: the skills it needed were scarce and getting scarcer. The company's response was to develop the Orange employee brand in line with its existing brand values, described as: simple, transparent, honest, fun, friendly, innovative and different. The idea was to position KPN Orange as a 'different employer' where the employee is as important as the customer. This involved creating a fun working environment that satisfied the rational and emotional needs of employees, and developing innovative benefits, including bonus opportunities for everyone, child care facilities, a laundry service, gym, massage, in-house banking, pizza delivery and a bus shuttle service for staff. Recruitment advertising campaigns built on the brand image and proved highly successful. KPN Orange successfully grew its headcount in Belgium from 50 employees in June 1998 to well over 1000 permanent staff in 2001.

The link with corporate brands

Many of the respondents in The Conference Board's survey saw the employer and corporate brand as one and the same thing. This is also the experience of Andrea Burrows, Managing Director of recruitment advertising and branding specialist AIA. 'I can't think of any client that doesn't believe in one brand,' she says. 'The employer brand is a sub-brand, but you can break the employer brand down into the same elements as you would a corporate brand.'

For example, imagine a fast food outlet. Its corporate brand can be divided into functional, economic and psychological elements as follows:

- *Functional:* it offers a range of well-known, branded burgers of consistent quality no matter where the outlet.
- *Economic:* low price food seen as good value.
- *Psychological:* a friendly place to go for all the family.

In employer branding terms, the functional element relates to the jobs offered, the training and working environment; the economic element relates to pay and benefits; and the psychological element could relate to the sense of belonging to a team, the emotional benefits of working for the organisation. The ways in which these brand elements are interpreted needs to be consistent with the corporate brand, yet also appealing to employees. This can sometimes be slightly problematic. For example, low priced food could be interpreted in employer branding terms as suggestive of a low cost organisation, and therefore a low wage employer. The fast food chain may need to put some effort into creating an attractive employer brand as follows:

- *Functional*: employees receive consistent training and development opportunities, no matter in which part of the organisation they work.
- *Economic*: pay and benefits are competitive and benchmarked to reflect market norms.
- *Psychological*: a friendly, supportive working environment.

Unilever is one organisation that has recognised the value to be gained from developing an employer brand. As a global business, Unilever has been working on a global brand to encompass what it stands for, its position in the market and what it has to offer its employees. The employer brand is seen as a vital element not only in recruiting people – future leaders and business transformers – to join the global group, but also in re-recruiting those who have already joined, increasing the chance that key employees will be retained. Terry Nolan, Senior Management Development Manager at Unilever, says: 'You have to remember that you don't just recruit someone once; you recruit them and then you re-recruit them every day or every week. That's why you need an employer brand, because people have a choice; once they decide psychologically that, "This is probably not the place for me any more", then it's very difficult to get them back.'

Coherent management practices

Success attracts success. Talented people will be attracted to organisations with clear strategic direction, supported by clearly aligned procedures. This means that recruitment cannot be separated from other operational functions of the business.

Terry Nolan, Senior Management Development Manager at Unilever, appreciates this state of affairs. 'The best people will be attracted and will stay in businesses which have clear strategies and aligned implementation. For example, if your strategy is to grow the top line, then you better make sure your remuneration systems reward that; lots of businesses do not reconcile their pay and incentives system with their strategic objectives in the market.' If there is a lack of alignment between strategy and implementation processes, high performers will understand that sustained business success is unlikely. The best people are winners; they do not want to be part of a mediocre business.

'The second thing that the best people look for is whether organisations seriously address poor performance,' Terry Nolan says. 'The best people thrive on the challenge and stimulus of other top quality performers. The evidence is that they abandon companies where poor performance is tolerated.'

One of the best-known examples of a company that refuses to tolerate poor performance is US giant, General Electric. Jack Welch, recently retired CEO, called it 'tough love'. General managers were required to rank all their people from one downwards, and each year the bottom 10% were fired. This may sound tough, but high achievers love it and will be more attracted to the organisation as a result. We consider the process of terminating employment contracts in Chapter 18: Firing.

Building coherent recruitment advertising campaigns

If you want to advertise to attract applications, tying your adverts closely to existing brand advertising can be highly effective.

One of Robert Half International's most successful recruitment campaigns was for Guinness, at a time when the brewing company had been running a highly successful 'Pure Genius' product advertising campaign. Guinness had spent huge sums on it, but as a result, the phrase 'pure genius' had become indelibly associated with the dark drink with the frothy white top.

Now, the Robert Half team wanted to tap into this success with the recruitment drive and found the perfect answer: placing job advertisements with the banner 'In search of pure genius'. It was simple, powerful and extremely effective. That campaign probably cost Guinness not more than £10,000, but they got the benefit of a multi-million pound brand advertising campaign behind it. We consider recruitment advertising in more detail in Chapter 9: Effective Advertising.

Recruiting as a marketing function

The relationship between the recruitment and marketing functions is not a one-way process; recruiting activity can itself be used to strengthen an organisation's brand image and profile.

For example, it may not always be necessary to advertise a new vacancy or number of new posts. However, placing a series of advertisements can be a means of putting the organisation's name out in the marketplace. Advertisements linked to expansion suggest an organisation is thriving. It is a good news story. Recruitment advertising can therefore reinforce the corporate brand, in the same way that the corporate brand reinforces the employer brand and the recruiter's appeal.

Similarly, the professionalism with which the recruitment process is handled can impact on the overall corporate brand. This means that each and every job application must be treated with the same professionalism as if it were the only one received. This includes responding quickly, making sure the recruitment process is fair and perceived to be fair and letting those people who do not make the grade down gently.

Even if 99% of these applicants lack the key skills required by the employer, all of them must be treated in a way that leaves them still wanting to work for the organisation. You want them to give a favourable report to their friends, family, colleagues and neighbours – anyone who may just be the person you *do* want in your workforce.

If rejected candidates give a bad report of your organisation, you might not only be losing a potential future employee; a bad experience of the recruitment process could also lose you a customer. If someone has had a look inside the organisation and found its systems lacking in efficiency or simple human courtesy, that could persuade them to take their custom elsewhere. Recruitment is therefore a key element in an organisation's successful reputation management processes.

Strategic selection

At the beginning of this chapter we identified attraction and selection as the two key elements of the recruitment process. In a sense, the selection process is itself a part of the attraction game. An organisation that has a reputation for success in selecting the most able people, and for the fairness and user-friendliness of the process, will find that it continues to attract talent. Appropriate selection procedures can therefore play a major part in reinforcing an employer brand and a reputation as an employer of choice.

Defining competencies

Effective selection must begin with identifying the qualities and characteristics of individuals most likely to succeed in the organisation and the role in question. Attitudes and behaviours are key. By developing a competency framework covering all the key roles in the organisation, employers have a clear guide as to what they are looking for in candidates.

Unilever has itself developed a competency framework. However, Terry Nolan recognises that desired competencies can change with the economic climate and the organisation's strategic aims. He explains: 'The thing about competencies is that the behaviours required by an organisation change depending on the agenda. If the top leadership team's strategy is global expansion and growth of market share and brand, then they will behave in a different way to a company whose strategy is survival. So the work we have been doing is to say that, this is the behaviour we need to achieve our current strategy. If the strategy changes, then it will be different. So you need people who have not just got the technical skills, but who have also got the behavioural flexibility to say, "OK, now we need to do something different." '

Appropriate selection tools

Once the qualities desired in candidates have been identified, recruiters need to select the appropriate selection techniques to identify and verify them.

The interview remains the most common section tool, although many organisations do not make the best of it. We consider effective interviewing techniques in Chapter 11: Interviewing: Technique Tips, and Chapter 12: Interviewing: Effective Questioning.

Combining the interview with other selection techniques maximises the recruiter's chance of success. Aptitude and skill tests and personality questionnaires can provide invaluable extra information for recruiters, as we consider in Chapter 13: Testing Times.

Creating a recruitment culture

Organisations that place recruitment high on the business agenda are most likely to succeed in the war for talent. Creating a recruitment culture means considering recruitment issues as part of any strategic business planning.

Recruitment has to be made a top priority by the people at the top. Michael Dell of Dell Computer Corporation is known for making people his company's top priority. He exhorts all of his managers to 'relentlessly recruit and hire world-class people'.

Organisations with a recruitment culture take every opportunity for sourcing new talent and see it as a continuous process. They build up a 'talent bank' that they can draw on as and when they need.

Building up a talent bank

Let us imagine you are an organisation that has understood the importance of attraction and created an employer brand.

However, when you receive speculative applications – which you do frequently – you do not make the best use of them. All you do is compare whether the person contacting you has skills suitable to any current vacancies. If not, you discard the individual's details, and send a polite rejection notice.

Could you use this information better? Anyone who contacts the organisation speculatively has one strong characteristic in their favour – they want to work for you. Could it be possible that this person may have skills that could be used in future, or that could be valuable now even though no actual vacancy has been identified? HR teams need to start thinking creatively about how they can use the people who apply to them.

As a starting point, organisations could keep hold of the contact details of people who conceivably would be suitable employees. Database technology makes it possible to keep efficient records of such speculative applications, enabling quick and easy searches to be run in future.

Given the demand for key skills, organisations could consider routinely interviewing speculative applicants who they think have talent to offer. HR and heads of functions should consider interviewing perhaps one person a week, depending on the level of speculative applications and the demand for new talent in the organisation. Talking through an individual's experience and identifying their competencies may identify a way in which their skills can be immediately useful to the organisation. Even if there are no openings available, the recruiter has extra information for the database.

Building up a talent bank in this way may enable future recruitment to be significantly speeded up, or even enable a vacancy to be filled without having to advertise it or involve a recruitment consultancy. At the least the recruiter will gain valuable information on how the organisation is perceived amongst potential recruits, why it appeals and how it compares with competitors.

Apart from speculative applicants, other candidates for the talent bank would include unsuccessful applicants to an advertised vacancy. These people may have talent, but perhaps someone just a little more suitable pipped them to the job offer. Nevertheless, they could still be attractive employees at a later date.

Similarly, recruiters should keep hold of details of applicants who turn down an offer of employment. An applicant may be dissuaded from accepting an offer by personal factors, economic uncertainty or the recruiter's inability to offer a sufficiently attractive package of pay and benefits at that time. It may be that the candidate simply had a better offer from elsewhere.

These reasons do not mean, however, that the candidate would not consider joining the organisation at a future date. Dr Gareth Jones, formerly Director of HR and Internal Communications at the BBC, says: 'I try to end the process as friends. I say, "I am really sorry we couldn't do a deal this time, Jeff. I really have enjoyed speaking with you over the last three months. Why don't we arrange to have a drink in six weeks, and you can let me know how the new job is going?" You never know. They may find they have made a mistake, but if you don't end as friends they will never phone you up again.'

Harnessing the power of technology

This book does not seek to give a complete picture of all the latest IT developments that HR departments can use when recruiting. However, using technology effectively can significantly enhance the process of creating a recruitment culture within the organisation.

For example, a company's website can be transformed into a powerful online career centre. Jobhunters attracted to your organisation by your corporate and employer brand can use the website to learn more about the working life there, as well as finding out about current vacancies. In addition, current employees can easily see what internal vacancies exist, encouraging them to think about career development *within* rather than outside the organisation. Recruitment consultants Executive Connections note this advantage in their guide to recruitment on the web, 'Mouse Hunting'. They write: 'Enabling existing employees to see what other opportunities are on offer within your organisation can mean that employees who otherwise might move see an opportunity which interests them and are thus encouraged to stay within your company.' We consider the process of advertising vacancies online in Chapter 9: Effective Advertising.

However, technology can do much more than this in helping to streamline the selection process. For example, human capital management and e-business specialist Kenexa has developed a wide range of IT solutions for recruiting, training and retaining talent. The technology can be used not only to conduct online assessments of candidates' skills and behaviours; it can also be used to search out CVs that candidates have posted on their own and third-party websites, so identifying potential applicants who might not otherwise have got in contact. In addition, Kenexa's interactive voice recognition (IVR) technology enables applicants to be pre-screened by telephone. Using a touch-tone phone, candidates respond yes or no to a series of practical and factual questions that typically concern educational qualifications, skills and availability for work. The approach increases efficiency in selection in the same way that e-based systems do, but does not rely on applicants having Internet access.

Employers who make use of technology effectively see significant benefits. Professional services firm KPMG has developed an online recruitment system, Global Successor, and as a result is saving 14 days on its previous hiring time. The system's features include managing job applications from all sources, including agencies and direct applications. CVs can be 'mined' for key data, interviews arranged via e-mail and psychometric tests conduced online.[4]

Organisations with strong recruitment cultures are prepared to experiment and adapt their recruitment practices. They do not just follow the usual channels when trying to bring in new talent. Instead they make the most of alternative routes into the talent pool, an approach we consider further in the next chapter.

Chapter 4

Alternative Sourcing

So many recruitment problems are self-inflicted. If you are a typical employer the chances are that, if you picture what you think you are looking for, you will come up with the following: a young, white, probably male, full-time, standard hours worker.

If you did not, please accept our apologies. But that may mean you are not that young, or not that white or not that male … The truth is that most of us have a natural tendency to recruit people like us with the unfortunate result that organisations miss out on so much talent.

When organisations cannot easily find the people they need, they need to make sure they are not cutting themselves off from tapping any potential talent pools, even unconsciously. After that, it is time to think more creatively about where to find potential new recruits.

Widening the pool

Some, if not all, employers create their own recruitment problems by maintaining too blinkered a view of who might be suitable employees, where they might be found and how they might be attracted.

If you as an employer are struggling to find the talent you need to drive the business forward, consider whether you are imposing limitations on yourself in terms of the people you consider when recruiting. Are you being too rigid about requiring formal qualifications for roles which may not need them? Could you instead test aptitude to establish a candidate's suitability for a given role?

Consider whether any particular groups are under-represented in your organisation, including:

- ethnic minorities;
- women;
- older workers;
- people with disabilities;
- part-timers.

In the UK it is illegal to discriminate against individuals on the grounds of race, sex or disability, and age discrimination is set to become illegal in 2006, in line with a European Commission directive. However, organisations should be looking beyond legal issues and recognising that encouraging internal diversity is not only a means for resolving talent shortages, but also a sensible commercial policy. Employers are increasingly recognising that there are benefits in establishing a workforce that more closely represents the organisation's client base. If you want to sell products and services to old and young, black and white, men and women, able and disabled, you are more likely to do so successfully if you understand the needs of each section of society. What better way to do that than to have members of all these sections on the in-house team?

If an organisation is under-represented in certain areas then there may be a need to review the organisation's culture or its recruitment and employment practices. Are there any aspects which, even unintentionally, may be putting certain people off?

In terms of culture, for example, if there are no women on the board or in top management positions, this could be sending negative signals to current and potential female employees about their chances of promotion in what may be perceived as an old boys type of organisation. Even if promotional chances are just as good, some women may decide that they would simply prefer to work in a more evenly balanced environment, where the culture is less 'blokish'.

As for the recruitment process, are the tests being used even-handed in distinguishing between people from different ethnic backgrounds? Or is there some bias in favour of white, middle class applicants? Have the people conducting interviews been trained not to let their first impressions dominate their final decision? First impressions can be determined by how similar the candidate appears to be to ourselves, a factor which may bear no relation to their suitability for the vacant position.

In terms of employment practices, how flexible is the organisation about allowing flexi-working or part-time options, which may appeal to people with families or older workers? Are such options discussed when new positions are being filled? Would it be possible for some employees to work from home, supported by IT in the form of laptops PCs and Internet links?

Similarly, people with disabilities can be overlooked when they would be able to do a job just as well as anyone else. Some people may be effectively ruled out because of restricted wheel-chair access. Thinking about such issues long-term, so that access issues are considered during any refurbishment work, for example, can gradually help to create a culture which recognises talent wherever it can be found.

As for part-timers, few organisations ever spare a thought about how they could tap into this source of extremely valuable talent. Part-time workers are generally never considered when organisations have a recruitment need, but they often have much to offer. Not only do many part-time workers have high levels of skills and expertise, they are often even more committed to their employers than full-timers, recognising that not everyone will give them a job. The irony is, of course, that many employers assume that part-time workers suffer from a lack of commitment, simply because they do not want to be working five days a week.

Elaine Howe co-founded Working Options, an employment agency focused entirely on part-time workers, in 1999. She had previously spent 10 years as an international finance manager for a multimedia company, before taking a two and a half year career break to look after her children. Howe wanted to resume her career part-time, but found that established employment agencies were unable to deliver. So she set up her own agency instead. Working Options has found a strong demand for part-time work from finance professionals, lawyers, marketing and

PR experts. However, employers have been generally slower to respond to the part-time option.

Elaine Howe says: 'There still needs to be a culture change. The big problem is that part-time people are seen as having a lack of commitment, because they are not there every day. However, the people who register with us who want to work part-time are generally very experienced and have excellent CVs. They are just looking for that work–life balance. It isn't necessarily to do with having children, nor is it a women's issue. A lot of people, for example, want to do some further studying, such as completing an MBA.'

Unusual pools

If traditional recruitment practices aimed at the general pool of local workers is proving insufficient to meet the organisation's need, other options could include:

- looking overseas;
- targeting MBA (Master of Business Administration) graduates;
- setting up an employee referral scheme;
- asking new recruits about talented former colleagues; or
- drawing on alumni networks.

Looking overseas

It may be that the specific skills required are in particular demand in the local marketplace. If so, what about attracting applicants from overseas?

Employers in continental Europe are generally better than their UK counterparts at appreciating the talents of overseas applicants. Although the UK is improving, many organisations remain relatively parochial in outlook.

However, as use of the Internet continues to grow, so advertising vacancies to people based in other countries becomes easier than ever. Employers wanting to try this route could highlight that applicants from different nationalities will be welcomed, and outline any relocation support that will be available. As the organisation gains a reputation for having an international outlook, so it is likely to attract even more applications from people outside the home base.

Targeting MBA graduates

Organisations are often looking for people with a mix of intellectual ability, an understanding of strategic issues and demonstrable practical experience. But how to find them? It can feel like looking for needles in haystacks.

However, such people are increasingly attracted to business schools to complete MBAs. They generally have some years of business experience under their belts, which they draw on in the classroom and in completing special projects for their degree.

These are potential leaders of the future, people who often have high expectations of their working lives and who are looking for new challenges. They may be the business transformers that the employer is looking for. Therefore, establishing links with business schools and marketing the career opportunities offered within your organisation may be a direct way of tapping into new talent pools.

However, there are a couple of potential downsides. First, people who complete MBAs will often be looking to make a step-change in their careers afterwards. They may be looking for a significant increase in responsibility compared with the last management role they held. Employers may have to take a certain leap of faith that the individual will be up to the job. Secondly, some MBA graduates have inflated salary expectations, perhaps understandably if they have paid for their own course and so have seen it as an investment in their own future. Therefore, there may be a need for robust salary negotiations and perhaps creative packages that build in bonuses based on performance.

Employee referral schemes

There is nothing new about the idea of employee referral schemes. Some organisations may have tried them and abandoned them for failing to deliver results. However, the point is that few organisations manage their employee referral schemes effectively.

In order to make such schemes work, employers need to explain clearly how the scheme operates to every new joiner. They then need to maintain awareness by regular reminders and particularly, by publicising any successful recruitment achieved through the scheme.

Last, but certainly not least, the rewards paid to staff who introduce a new recruit need to be sufficiently attractive to make it worth those people's time putting in the effort to think about people they could introduce. One top law firm pays a bonus of £10,000 to staff who introduce a new recruit to the organisation. It is a large enough sum to create strong interest in the referral scheme, but still highly cost efficient when compared to other recruiting methods such as advertising.

One advantage of running such a scheme is that people who already work for you will have a good idea of what it takes to be successful in the organisation. They should, therefore, be likely to generate pretty good leads in terms of potential recruits. The people who join via this route are also likely to have a more realistic understanding of what working life there is like, since they will have heard about it firsthand through the contact who introduced them. Therefore, there is a greater chance that the fit between recruit and recruiter will be reasonably good and the expectations of both parties will be reasonable and will therefore be met.

Maintaining an effective employee referral scheme requires the commitment of the internal communications or marketing team, as well as support from HR. They will need to boost the scheme's profile, which can be achieved by circulating details of positions that need to be filled and by specifying the kinds of competencies required by those suitable to apply. Include gentle reminders that it is not just former colleagues who may be of interest, but impressive people they know through out-of-hours pastimes – the football club, skiing holiday group or local church.

Since nothing motivates people like success, make sure that news of any successful referrals – and bonuses paid out – are spread round the organisation to inspire others to come up with suggestions too. Be loud and proud of such scheme successes.

Asking new recruits

When a new employee joins you, this individual will have his or her own contact book – former colleagues in the organisation they have just left, or people they worked with some years previously but with whom they have stayed in touch. Therefore, if your organisation has talent shortages in certain areas, it may be worth having an informal chat to see whether the incoming recruit can suggest some people who may also be interested in joining.

Of course, a senior individual may be restricted by a non-solicitation clause in their previous employment contract with their former employer. Such clauses are designed to prevent them poaching colleagues, customers and even suppliers and are now common in most contracts, other than for employees at the lowest levels. Such clauses should be treated with sensitivity because a breach by the new employee may result in your organisation being held accountable, whether for inducing a breach of contract or for interfering with the other employer's economic or business interests. Such provisions are known to be hard to enforce, both because the clause itself must only go so far as is reasonable and necessary to protect an employer's legitimate business interests, and also due to the difficulty in obtaining the necessary evidence. Non-solicitation clauses that are drawn too widely, or apply in blanket fashion to poaching of all employees, customers or suppliers are unlikely to be enforceable.

As for negating a claim in respect of a former colleague who would be a great asset to an organisation, no such claim should arise if the former colleague responds to an advertisement for a vacancy made by the recruiting organisation. How such an advertisement comes to the attention of the former colleague may give rise to a claim, but may also be difficult to prove. Tread carefully in such situations and where appropriate, take legal advice.

Alumni networks

Few organisations run alumni programmes and when they do, their prime motive is often to generate future business, rather than as a potential source of future talent.

However, we have already noted the increasingly fluid nature of people's careers and working relationships in Chapter 2: The Candidate Agenda. Staff may leave an organisation for a variety of reasons – to achieve a faster promotion, to gain higher pay, to have greater variety of experience and so on. The reasons may not necessarily mean that the individual would never like to come back and work for the organisation again.

Of course, you may not want to take some people back, but there will always be certain individuals that the employer will be extremely sad to lose. Why lose contact with them? Why not stay in touch, formally and informally, just in case this person's personal job requirements change again in future?

Formal contact can be maintained by means of annual events and receptions where old colleagues can reunite over a drink and catch up on new developments. Alumni newsletters also provide a useful means of keeping leavers up to date with developments in the organisation, while circulating copies of the organisation's internal staff newsletter can make former employees feel they are still a part of the team. Sections of the corporate website can also be adapted for alumni, providing information on the organisation's development and on the progress of former colleagues.

Maintaining contact in this way may result in someone rejoining the organisation years after they first left. Sometimes people can be persuaded back sooner. The more the organisation can do to make it clear that an individual would be welcome back, the better. Most people, however wrongly, may feel that returning to an employer they left suggests they made a mistake in leaving. Even if they are told at their leaving interview 'We'd love to have you back if things don't work out', they still may find it too hard to pick up the phone and ask about returning.

At Robert Half International we made a point of easing any potential return. We identified the leavers we would really like to have back and then we treated them psychologically as if they were still part of the organisation. We continued to send them staff newsletters as well as the occasional personalised note with news of former colleagues and departmental successes. The lines of communication were kept open, and the message frequently given that they would be welcome back at any time. The technique proved successful. People found it easier to return if they could present it to contacts and colleagues as a case of being head-hunted back, rather than a result of things not working out elsewhere.

Sometimes people left and returned several times over. Such is the nature of the recruitment industry and at Robert Half we did not consider it a problem. It is better to have the benefit of able people on your team even temporarily than it is to lose them for good.

However, there are some times when you simply cannot find the permanent staff you need. What can employers do then? We consider some options in Chapter 5: Alternatives to Recruitment.

Alternatives to Recruitment

T his is a book about recruitment. However, it is also a book that tries to suggest solutions for organisations struggling to find the talent they need to thrive. Recruitment is one means to the end of accessing talent, but recruitment alone may not provide all the answers.

There are a number of alterative options that organisations may want to consider if recruitment appears unable to fulfil their skill needs. These could include:

- reducing staff losses;
- rethinking promotion policies;
- increasing use of internal transfers;
- re-skilling current employees;
- giving greater attention to succession planning;
- creating job-share and part-time opportunities;
- increasing use of interim or temporary personnel;
- outsourcing functions.

We assume here that organisations are not creating problems for themselves by trying to recruit when there is actually no need to do so. We consider the importance of identifying real recruitment needs in Chapter 7: The Recruitment Process. In this chapter we focus on practical steps that organisations can take when they really do have a talent shortage but recruitment cannot solve the problem.

Reducing staff losses

It is an obvious point, but one worth making, that organisations could reduce their recruitment problems if they reduced the rate at which existing staff leave.

As we have noted in Chapter 2: The Candidate Agenda, modern career builders – such as members of Generation X – expect to move between organisations at relatively frequent intervals. These days younger workers anticipate moving on to a new role after perhaps just 18 months to two years. Even older workers are starting to appreciate the benefits of portfolio careers and the potential rewards that can come from not tying yourself too closely to a single, lifetime employer. Therefore, organisations can expect on-going high staff turnover rates to be a normal fact of operational life.

The importance of re-recruitment

Even so, most organisations could do more to try to encourage staff to stay for longer. Leading edge organisations increasingly appreciate that once they have recruited a new member of staff, the attraction game is not over; they then need to re-recruit that individual on an on-going basis. This is such an important issue that we look at it in detail in Chapter 17: Re-recruitment.

The key point to understand is that people make one decision to join an employer; the subsequent decision to stay or go is an entirely separate one. Employers need to treat the two issues separately. There will of course be overlaps – someone may be attracted because they perceive an employer's culture as dynamic and supportive of talent; they may decide to stay for the same reason. However, people and organisational circumstances change. An individual may join a company because he or she wants lots of travel; they may later leave because they have had enough of spending time in airports and the employer has failed to offer them an alternative working lifestyle.

All the employer can do is to seek to understand the needs of employees on an on-going basis. This requires effective internal communication channels and a culture which supports people who challenge the norm. Decisions to stay or go will be based on numerous factors, including the extent to which the individual enjoys working with colleagues, the degree to which he or she feels suitably rewarded and the on-going challenges of the role. Some of these factors will be beyond the employer's control. However, years of recruiting suggests a particularly common reason that people give for seeking pastures new with a different employer – they did not really feel involved with the last one.

Inclusion appeal

Employers who work hard to create an inclusive culture generally do better at retaining staff. It is human nature for people to want to feel they 'belong'.

Ron Dennis, who runs the McLaren racing team, understands the needs for inclusion. He believes that the success of his drivers depends on a team effort by everyone associated with the team. If people are to give of their best, they need to feel involved in the outcome. But it is not possible for everyone in the wider team to be trackside during a race. So afterwards Ron holds a debriefing session attended by every single member of staff – from cleaners to canteen employees, from mechanics to designers. He delivers a blow-by-blow account of how the race went. In this way everyone feels like an insider, who knows what is going on, what needs to be improved and who shares in any successes.

Even when staff do decide to leave, organisations need to keep their tentacles locked onto key individuals. As discussed in the preceding chapter, keep in regular contact and treat leavers almost as if they had never left – keep up that inclusive approach and perhaps one day they may come back to you.

Rethinking promotion policies

Is promotion always vertical? If so, why?

Traditional hiring and employment strategies are up for interrogation. So are promotion policies. Historically organisations have worked on the basis that people progress by promotion up through the managerial ranks. The problem is someone may be good at their job, and then be promoted out of it to a managerial or administrative role that does not make the best use of their talents. This person may not actually want to make the change in role, but does so since this is the only way to achieve a promotion and an accompanying pay rise.

Organisations need to step out of this 'Catch 22' situation. Accept that this individual is a valuable asset to the organisation and great at what he does. So why not give him the pay rise and recognise his achievements, but allow him to carry on doing what he wants to do, which is actually what he does best? Organisations are in any case much flatter than they used to be, so there is not even room for everyone with talent to move up to the upper managerial reaches.

Increasing use of internal transfers

Promoting internal transfers, including international moves, can help to meet talent needs while incentivising employees. Say you have a member of staff who is fulfilling a valuable role in the organisation. She has enjoyed her work but has now been doing it for three years and is feeling the need for change. There are no obvious vertical promotions suitable. Left alone, there is a fair chance that this person will start looking for a new employer. The role she finds may be a similar one, but at least the environment and specific processes will be different.

As this person's employer it is your interest to try and keep her. One option is to look for similar roles that she could fulfil but perhaps in a different part of the organisation. Maybe she could swap roles with someone else? If she is offered the chance for new challenges, she may stay for several more years, enabling the organisation to continue tapping into her extensive knowledge. If the employer develops a reputation for promoting internal employee mobility, and makes this a part of its employer brand, it should even find knock-on benefits in terms of improved candidate appeal.

Re-skilling current employees

The key determinants of job performance are attitudes and behaviours. Certain skills, expertise, knowledge and qualifications may be necessary, but it is attitudes and behaviours that recruiters should really look out for. Ask managers what they look for in staff and the answer will often be, 'a can-do attitude'.

As an employer if you have an employee with the attitudes and behaviours that make them successful in your organisation you really do not want to let them go. This person is a known asset, and one that knows and understands your organisation. If their role becomes redundant, do not automatically say 'thank-you and good-bye'. What about offering the chance to retrain?

Most organisations have a skill shortage somewhere within them at any given time. Could this known and valued individual be transferred into one of these areas?

You could go out and try to recruit someone who has skills you need, but you will not really know about their behaviour and attitudes until they turn up at work and start performing, or not, as the case may be. There are no guarantees in recruiting.

One reason why some organisations fail to achieve the kind of internal mobility that would help ease their staffing shortages is that they have become too fixated on skills, experience and qualifications as essential requirements in candidates for certain jobs. Instead, they should focus more on competencies. So this managerial position has traditionally been filled by someone with a first degree and professional marketing qualifications. Are these both really necessary? Could someone else in the existing team be helped to develop existing competencies through carefully selected training courses?

Focused succession planning

Developing a culture that supports personal development, training and learning is a sensible strategy in its own right. Rather than having to recruit all top-level positions, it may be easier to recruit more junior, less experienced people and then train them up so that they can fill senior posts in a few years' time. As noted above, organisations that develop positive reputations for training and development will find it generally easier to recruit staff in the first place.

The most effective succession planning will be based around a competency framework that identifies the skills and behaviours required for success in certain positions. Training courses can then be developed around that framework to develop younger employees in appropriate ways. Organisations may worry that by investing in such training programmes they are making their employees more attractive to other employers. This is of course true, but it is no reason for not training staff. Employers who do not spend money on training will find it harder not only to recruit but also to retain the people they need.

Job-share and part-time potential

If an organisation is experiencing recruitment problems, it needs to consider creative solutions to solving its skill shortages. Take job-sharing as an example. How many organisations actively support job-sharing proposals? Very few indeed.

Job-sharing situations usually arise as a result of an existing member of staff wishing to move to a part-time contract without having to give up their role completely. It may be that there is an obvious other individual already within the organisation who could share the work. If not, the employer will need to go out and find another suitable part-time worker. Most are unwilling to do so, even though as we noted in the preceding chapter there is some excellent part-time talent available.

Employers may ask, what is in it for us? Why should we support job-sharing? If they have to recruit someone else anyway, they may be tempted to reject the job-share request, even if that means the incumbent employee leaves.

For starters, assuming the individual involved is a good performer, organisations benefit from retaining known achievers. Secondly, putting effort into trying to accommodate employee needs sends positive signals to everyone in the organisation that this is a good place to work. Thirdly, organisations that respond to employee needs by offering part-time and other flexible working options generally benefit from the resulting staff loyalty. It is a win–win situation for employer and employee. There will always be some posts for which job-sharing or part-time working is not feasible, but they are probably fewer in number than most employers assume. Organisations that try to avoid making assumptions about essential working practices will find fewer problems in maintaining the workforce talent they need.

Interim or temporary personnel

The 1990s saw a massive increase in the use of temporary personnel by organisations seeking to relieve short-term, or even long-term, staffing problems. There are many advantages from using temporary staff. For example:

- temporary personnel can be brought in at extremely short notice;
- organisations have greater flexibility in responding to peaks and troughs in demand;
- one-off projects – such as managing the integration of two business units or implementing a new IT system – can be handled efficiently, without taking on a permanent new member of staff;
- high-quality skills are available if needed, potentially beyond the skills the organisation could afford on a full-time permanent basis.

The temp market clearly contains many different types of people with varying levels of skills and experience. However, interim managers, at the top-end of the market, are often extremely experienced people. They have the experience that enables them to walk into an organisation and quickly understand the issues to be addressed. Some have chosen to work as interim managers as a lifestyle decision, since between projects they can take considerable time off. Others may have been made redundant and, due to their age, found less interest from employers in giving them permanent positions, whereas grey hairs are respected in the interim management marketplace. Some may have made money on corporate ventures, but still feel they have much to offer the business world. Any organisations that have never considered bringing in such people to work on specific projects could benefit significantly from doing so in future.

Resources Connection is a specialist in the interim arena, employing finance, HR and IT professionals to work on short- to medium-term projects for clients. The company has been operating successfully in the US for several years and opened up for business in London in September 2001. Resources' business model is somewhat different to that of traditional interim management agencies in that it employs the professionals instead of them operating through limited company vehicles. UK Director Bob Leach says: 'The increasingly project-based nature of much work makes the use of interim personnel highly appropriate. Our staff go in with a highly focused approach in order to get the job done. For example, past projects our staff have worked on have included providing regulatory framework guidance for a large investment bank, and providing analytical and decision support capability in a large personnel group which wanted to get a better handle on its cost base.' Other typical projects include the provision of interim financial controllers to cover for maternity leave and the management of IT implementations.

Outsourcing functions

So you have tried recruiting, you have tried looking for internal transfers and temps cannot meet your long-term needs. How about outsourcing?

Outsourcing is, in a sense, another form of accessing temporary resources. You can outsource short-term projects or whole departmental functions – IT services, accounting, HR and payroll management or facilities management, to name but a few suitable candidates.

The growth of outsourcing has followed from the business philosophy that it is best to stick to your knitting. If you are a widget manufacturer, anything apart from making those widgets is outside your core activity. You are not a specialist in it, but other people are.

The potential advantages of outsourcing are that the organisation can tap into specialist skills, for an agreed price. The organisation no longer has to worry itself about recruiting people with appropriate expertise to fulfil those functions, nor about providing the training and development needed to keep those people up to date. Your specialist service provider, however, by virtue of its specialist focus, should be able to provide the training and development opportunities required to attract top performers. Your organisation should benefit as a result.

Outsourcing will not suit all organisations, of course. For cultural issues some may prefer to keep on with the traditional model of maintaining in-house services. However, for organisations that have been struggling to recruit the resources they need, handing the problem over to an outsourcing specialist may be a solution worth considering.

In his book *The Elephant and the Flea*, Charles Handy envisages a world where elephants, the large employing organisations, and the fleas, independent workers, co-exist in mutually beneficial ways.[1] Your flea could be the major accountancy firm that provides outsourced financial accounting services, or your former colleague who now provides consultancy advice to a number of different organisations. Managing all these relationships effectively, and knowing how to tap into what external skills when, can enable organisations to operate as if they had a far higher headcount than they actually do.

Recruitment has its place; there will always be a need to recruit key talented people to sit at the core of any organisation. However, recruitment will not always be the answer for every organisation trying to meet every resourcing need.

Where it is, however, you need to do it as well as possible and avoid the common recruitment mistakes people make. We have a look at what not to do in Chapter 6: Common Recruitment Failings.

Chapter 6

Common Recruitment Failings

Recruiting is a difficult business and it is easy to make mistakes. Learning from other people's mistakes can save a lot of time and effort. Here is our list of common recruitment failings:

Errors of process
- Overlooking the business strategy.
- Failing to clarify what you are looking for.
- Using the wrong method.
- Rushing the decision.

Errors of attitude
- Looking for Superman and Superwoman.
- Pre-occupation with qualifications, skills and experience and, ignoring attitudes and behaviours.
- Recruiting people in your own image.
- Recruiting people in the image of the previous incumbent.

Errors of application
- Under-selling the opportunity.
- Over-selling.
- Giving candidates an inconsistent message.
- Ignoring emotion.

Errors of process

The recruitment mistakes in this group generally result from lack of effective planning. You cannot rush recruitment, not without risking a poor result.

Overlooking the business strategy

The need to recruit new talent into the organisation should always be viewed in a business context. Recruitment should be treated as an opportunity to review strategies – whether at an organisational, departmental or immediate team level.

Instead, too much recruitment is conducted as a knee-jerk reaction to someone's resignation letter. When a team member resigns, most people's automatic response is to set the recruitment wheels in motion straight away.

But do you really need to? Say this team member had joined the business at a time when it was going through a period of major expansion. His role had become primarily one of project management, co-ordinating in-house integration teams and external consultancies to ensure the development of a common IT platform and systems. However, much of this process has now been completed. In fact, part of the reason for this employee's resignation is that his role has become progressively less challenging, and he could see no route for further development.

The question is, do you really need to replace this individual with someone just like him? There is still some short-term integration work to be completed, but this may not require a full-time permanent employee to handle it. Perhaps you would be better off considering other options, such as identifying one of his colleagues who is looking for such experience and who has the potential to be able to handle the extra work. Alternatively, you could bring in an interim manager until the integration is finally complete. As another option, you could hand the responsibility for final co-ordination to one of the consultancies already involved.

Any of these options would avoid the organisation taking on a full-time employee at a time when the future workload is uncertain. Saving the leaver's salary would pay for the extra consultancy or interim support, or for a pay rise for the colleague who takes on some of his role, as well as achieving bottom-line departmental savings that will impress the IT director.

Failing to clarify what you are looking for

Recruitment consultants are used to somewhat panicked calls from client organisations explaining that they have got to replace so and so. But have they drawn up a job specification or a candidate profile? Surprisingly, too often the answer is that they have not.

Clarifying what you are looking for should follow on naturally from putting the recruitment need in a strategic business context. You have decided that you do need to bring in someone new to takeover from the leaving staff member, but the role will be modified slightly. You define the role to be filled in the job description, and then outline a candidate profile to describe the kind of person who could perform that role. We consider how to prepare these key recruiting documents in detail in Chapter 7: The Recruitment Process. Do not forget to identify the attitudes required to get on in the role, as well as the skills and experience.

Using the wrong method

The recruitment method chosen needs to suit the vacancy in terms of level and sector. If you are looking for a middle manager, you probably do not need to pay head-hunting fees. An advertised selection process should do the trick. However, if you are trying to fill a senior position, requiring someone with rare skills in a niche industry sector, you may well need to mount a targeted search, handled by a head-hunter, to find your man or woman.

Since some recruitment consultancies have greater expertise in selection, and others in search, you need to check that you appoint the right one to handle the vacancy. We consider this issue in detail in Chapter 8: Calling in the Cavalry: Recruitment Consultancies.

More subtle errors of methodology could involve placing an advertisement on the wrong day or in the wrong publication, or failing to allow Internet job searchers to e-mail in their applications. We address how to avoid some of these errors in Chapter 9: Effective Advertising.

Rushing the decision

Okay, so there is a war for talent going on. There are other people out there trying to snap up the best people, in just the same way you are. But that does not mean you have to jump to a candidate's tune unless you are certain about your decision. Nor should you have to move before you are ready because of pressure from powers that be above you. Recruiting can go seriously wrong this way.

Dr Gareth Jones, formerly Director of HR and Internal Communications at the BBC, says: 'You do sometimes get pressured by your boss. "Haven't we filled that marketing job yet?" I will explain that I am not certain and that I need to get more data. I won't be rushed. Similarly, you will occasionally feel rushed by pressure of the labour market. A candidate may say, "Unless I hear from you tomorrow I'm going to take that job with BA." Well the truth probably is that BA hasn't actually offered a job yet. Once in a while you will lose out, but it's better to hold your nerve and just wait until you have got enough data to make your decision.'

Errors of attitude

Errors of attitude can occur even when organisations have reasonable recruitment processes in place. They result from allowing personal preferences or mistaken attitudes to the recruitment process to get in the way.

Looking for Superman and Superwoman

It goes without saying that if you look for perfection, you will not find it. Organisations can get carried away when drawing up the candidate profile and include a load of qualifications and characteristics that simply go beyond the needs of the job and the likely pay package to be offered. Recruitment has to be undertaken with a sense of realism at its heart.

Being realistic begins with the job description and candidate profile. Identify the 'must have' features and the 'nice to haves'. Remember that the recruitment process almost always involves an element of compromise between the aims of the candidate and the preferences of the organisation. The candidate is usually looking for a new job because he or she wants a new challenge, the chance to learn new skills or apply them in new ways. Meanwhile, recruiting organisations would usually prefer to employ someone who has done exactly the same job as the one they are filling, in an organisation as similar to their own as possible.

If the recruiter and the candidate are to meet in the middle, both parties need to be a little flexible. The recruiting organisation has to understand that some aspect of the job may be new to the candidate, but that this should inspire and excite them. The candidate has to accept that there needs to be some crossover of their skills, otherwise they would not be applying for the job in the first place. Recruiters who remember this two-way deal will have more success that those who try to ignore it.

Looking for Superman is not only problematic in terms of simply being impossible, it also suggests that the organisation has failed to identify what it is really looking for. It may be that the person you offer the job to is not actually the 'best' candidate. The person who appears to be the best may actually be over-qualified for this position; if you appoint them there is a risk they may become bored, do shoddy work and end up moving on fast. This person may perhaps be worth considering for some other role in the organisation if they have skills that are in demand, but for the immediate vacancy the ideal appointment may actually be someone with apparently lesser skills.

Pre-occupation with qualifications, skills and experience, and ignoring attitudes and behaviours

Employers often focus on the qualifications that they want their recruits to have, the skills and experience that they can demonstrate. Clearly some qualifications and certain skills are essential for certain jobs. However, the emphasis on qualifications, skills and experience often comes at the expense of attention given to attitudes and behaviours.

Research shows that it is attitudes and behaviours that have the main impact on career success. Employers could therefore improve the results of their recruitment activities – as demonstrated by the actual performance of their new joiners once they are on board – by remembering to investigate the attitudes and behaviours of job candidates, as well as their qualifications, skills and experience.

Recruiting people in your own image

One of the most basic mistakes of recruiting is recruiting people in your own image. It is also a mistake that could seriously limit your organisation's creative dynamism. It can happen when there is an inadequate job description or candidate profile, or when these are being ignored.

This is, of course, an extremely human mistake to make. You read a candidate's CV and realise that you both studied the same subject at college, like the same music and both have an interest in pot-holing. Amazing! Even better, this candidate started her career in the same company that you did. What a coincidence! You are, naturally, already predisposed in this candidate's favour and the interview just confirms your gut feel that she is a 'good thing'. Okay, she does not have quite as much management experience as that other applicant, but ...

Now, appointing the candidate you share so much with could still be the right decision; but not just because you recognise a like soul. The candidate should justifiably get the job if she is the most appropriate applicant. Recruiting someone because they appear similar to you is understandable. You think you understand how they tick; you feel extremely comfortable in their presence.

However, diversity in a team can help to generate creative thought. You may also be able to deliver a better service because the team encompasses a wider range of views, representing those of a broader cross-section of the community.

Recruiting people in the image of the previous incumbent

This results from making the assumption that if a certain kind of person was doing the job before, then a similar person needs to be recruited to do it now. It ignores the fact that the job could have changed since the last person took it on.

Think about your business needs. Sit down with the last incumbent, and with colleagues on the team, to identify exactly what you need the new recruit to do. Do not just dig out and dust down the old job specification that was used last time. By all means use it as a starting point, but make sure you update it to reflect the here and now.

Errors of application

The processes and attitudes for successful recruitment may be in place, but things can still go wrong in the application and spoil your recruitment plans.

Under-selling the opportunity

Recruiting can go seriously wrong if the recruiting organisations assume they are calling all the shots. As an interviewer, or as a member of the HR team planning the recruitment campaign, it is good to have pride in your organisation and to believe that other people would enjoy working there. However, you cannot assume everyone will see things your way. You have to sell your belief to the candidates. Make sure they know all the advantages.

These days every organisation has to sell itself. What is in it for the candidate? Why should someone with several opportunities open to them take this job? This aspect has to be considered right from the job specification through to the advert, when briefing recruitment consultants and when preparing for interviews.

Effective selling can also only be done with an understanding of the candidate's agenda. As we discussed in Chapter 2: The Candidate Agenda, Generation X and Y applicants may have different expectations and wish lists from people a couple of generations older.

The sales message has to be tailored to the kind of person you think the job is suited for. Details about the job may be the same; it may just be that certain aspects of the organisation's culture are highlighted, or the pay and benefits package is tweaked to offer different elements. You need to make sure the sales message gets those niceties across.

Selling at its simplest involves treating the candidate with consideration, courtesy and openness from the moment contact is made. That includes responding promptly to applications, giving feedback on performance in tests and interviews and always being polite. Small details can have a big impression when competing for talent against rivals who pay less attention to the little things.

Over-selling

Although as a recruiter you need to sell the opportunity, you must not lose your sense of reality. Yes, you want to attract some top talent; yes, you want to persuade your most suitable candidate to accept the job offer; but you must not try to tempt them in by creating a false expectation of what the role, the opportunity, or the culture in the organisation is really like. To be truly successful, recruiting has to be based on honesty. Selling someone the world, when all they are going to get is a little piece of Essex, will result in major disillusionment for your newest recruit.

Over-selling could actually put people off. The best approach is to be enthusiastic about all the good stuff, but be honest about the tougher parts. Admit that the travelling can be perhaps too demanding in the winter months, but explain that you do get extra days off if you have to travel at weekends. Present the job and the organisation in the round.

Giving candidates an inconsistent message

Consider this example: a blue-chip company was wanting to recruit quality people to join its internal audit department. Now, this is not the sexiest job role in the world, as any recruiter will tell you. To get quality applicants, you have got to come up with an attractive message, a 'what is in it for you' to get people applying. The recruitment consultant spoke to a senior manager in the internal audit team who was closely involved in the recruitment drive and who understood this need for a strong hook.

This manager suggested a number of selling points: first, that the department had high visibility, allowing its members extensive access to extremely senior people in the organisation; secondly, that time in internal audit usually included a period of secondment elsewhere in the organisation, and so provided really meaty experience; and thirdly, that time in internal audit should be seen as a transition period, leading on to other things within the organisation – people should only expect to spend between two and three years there, maximum. This was the future situation that the manager wanted to see developing in the department and he wanted to recruit people on that basis.

The recruiter liked this angle, and used the three-pronged appeal to sell the position to candidates. His recommended short-list of candidates then had a first-round interview with the senior manager, who reinforced this message and continued to inspire interest in the candidates. Final interviews were then held with the head of the internal audit department. The candidates naturally asked him about the potential to move on in a couple of years. The head was incredulous. 'No one has ever moved on in three years,' he replied.

End of recruitment story. Candidates were immediately put off, not just because their initial hopes of using the role as a launch pad to other, sexier things had been dashed; they also lost faith in an organisation that had given such a confused message.

The moral of this story is that recruiting employers have to get their sales message straight, one that relates to the candidate's likely agenda, and then they have to make sure that everyone involved in the recruitment and selection process buys into that message. This does not just apply to specific aspects of a particular vacant role, but also to the culture and opportunities offered by the organisation itself. The message given to candidates needs to be consistent with the overall employer brand, an idea we explore in more depth in the next chapter.

Ignoring emotion

When recruiting, interviewers must remember that they do not have to become best friends with the recruit; they just have to be confident that the individuals will fit into the team and work effectively there. So the absence of a highly positive 'click' should not be seen as a problem.

That said, gut feeling should not be ignored totally. If you have a strong negative feeling about a candidate, then it is probably unwise to offer that person the job. An emotional or gut feeling could be giving you valuable information. Do not ignore it completely.

However, you must be sure that your gut feeling is not just a symptom of unjustifiable prejudices or subconscious pre-judgements. In Chapter 11: Interviewing: Technique Tips, we consider effective interviewing and emphasise how common it is for people to make decisions about a person within minutes of meeting them. Make sure you give every candidate a fair hearing. Listen to what they are really saying and watch how they actually behave, rather than interpreting their words and actions in the hazy light of your own misconceptions.

Having considered what can go wrong with recruitment, in Part II: Practical Recruiting, we move on to look at the attraction and selection process in detail. Our aim is to provide practical advice to maximise your chances of achieving recruiting excellence.

Part II

Practical Recruiting

Chapter 7

The Recruitment Process

Y ou need talent to drive your organisation forward, but how are you going to get it? We hope you are building an employer brand, as discussed in Chapter 3: Strategies for Successful Recruitment, but you still need an effective recruitment process. The recruitment process will itself impact on the success and strength of your employer brand. So, whether you are an HR expert or a line manager with a vacancy to fill, this chapter should help make sure you do recruit effectively.

Identifying recruitment needs: is there a vacancy at all?

Recruitment may be triggered by the organisation's expansion or by the decision to move in a new strategic direction, requiring the influx of additional skills and fresh talent. In such cases, the need for the recruitment drive may be relatively clear.

However, much recruitment occurs as a result of a knee-jerk reaction in response to a member of staff handing in their notice. Whenever an existing member of staff resigns, the line manager's instinctive reaction will be: 'Jeff has resigned; so let's recruit another Jeff.'

Stop! As we noted in Chapter 3: Strategies for Successful Recruiting, this is one of the commonest recruitment mistakes. Jeff may have been excellent at his job, but you have to ask some basic questions before taking any action. Does a vacancy really exist? If it does, does that mean we still need another Jeff?

Whenever an existing staff member resigns, the line manager should take time to look at the role the individual was filling and reaffirm that there is still an on-going need for it. Take the opportunity to perform a strategic review of the team or department in which the role sits, and consider how it interacts with the other roles around it.

Questions to consider are as follows:

- What is the purpose of this role?
- How does the role help the organisation to achieve its strategic goals?
- What value does it add to the team?
- How does it relate to the roles of colleagues?
- What reason has been given for the resignation?
- Has the nature of the role changed recently? If so how?
- Should the role be reduced in future, or expanded?
- Can the person be persuaded to stay?

The answers will help to indicate the appropriate response. For example, it may be that the role has fallen in importance due to technological advances which have lowered the value or need for human involvement. Perhaps the business has been changing its strategic direction so that a role that was once key to its success is now relatively unimportant. The fact that the role has shrunk in importance may actually have triggered the staff member's resignation. Of course, even if the role appears to have lost importance, that does not necessarily mean it can be ignored altogether.

If the role could be expanded in some areas to make it more valuable, that may even be sufficient to persuade the incumbent to stay on, attracted by the new challenges involved.

Therefore, before leaping straight to a decision to recruit, the line manager, together with HR, should consider a range of alternative options. Specific options will clearly be determined by the specific circumstances involved. However, these could include:

- dividing the role between existing members of staff, provided they have some spare capacity to be able to absorb it;
- bringing in part-time help to cover the staffing need;
- moving another individual into the role, perhaps someone who has expressed the desire for a change of activity and who has the appropriate skills or development potential; or
- expanding the role to take on new responsibilities more closely linked to the organisation's strategic direction, and so persuading the incumbent to stay on.

The result of such considerations may be that a different, perhaps more junior role, is the one that needs to be filled, or that a different type of role (part-time) may need to be created, or that a more highly specialised role needs to be created in future. Whatever the outcome, such an assessment will ensure that any resulting recruitment is founded on a true business need.

Defining the role to be filled: the job description

The process of verifying the recruitment need is a useful first step in analysing precisely what role needs to be filled, and so what competencies the successful applicant will need to possess. The results of the analysis of desired competencies can then be summarised in a job description.

A typical job description should cover a number of key issues:

- the organisation's profile;
- the position's overall purpose and context;
- specific priorities and objectives of the role;
- reporting lines;
- responsibilities.

The organisation's profile
This should be a high level review focusing on:

- key markets;
- strategic goals and future direction,
- recent significant developments,
- the prevailing culture and the perceived management style – key elements of the employer brand.

This information should be self-evident if those in the organisation have a clear sense of purpose. However, if questions of culture or management style are unclear, this may suggest that the HR team should undertake some internal research to gain a more focused understanding of how current employees perceive the organisation. Why do people enjoy working there? Why do they stay? Why do they leave? This should be an on-going process, drawing on feedback from leavers and from new recruits, as well as through communication with employees who remain with the organisation for long periods.

The position's overall purpose and context

The job description should outline how the role fits into the organisation's strategic objectives. Why is this role needed in the organisation? How does the position contribute to the success of the organisation? (One way to answer these questions is to consider what would happen if the role did not exist. Of course, if the answer is 'nothing', then you should wonder why you are recruiting at all.) Include an explanation of how the role relates to other roles and to other departments within the organisation.

Specific priorities and objectives of the role

This is where the job description starts to get detailed. What exactly is the function of this role? What will the person who fills it be doing?

Reporting lines

Who does the role report to?
Who reports to the person filling this role?

Responsibilities

This should not simply be a list of duties. It should, however, specify what tasks are completed by the role and how much authority the individual will have within the organisation. It should also indicate the standards that will be expected in the completion of those tasks.

Try to emphasise the potential benefits for the candidate in taking the position. Although the focus will be on 'What is in it for the organisation?', as far as a potential applicant is concerned, the key issue will be 'What is in it for me?'. Perhaps the role will involve significant exposure to top management, or involvement with functions throughout the organisation so that the individual will develop a strong sense of commercial operations. Spelling out such benefits in the job description should make it easier for all those involved in the recruitment process to communicate clearly why this is a job worth taking.

Figure 7.1 shows a sample job description for a vacant position at fictional company Books Plus Select.

BOOKS PLUS SELECT: JOB DESCRIPTION

Job Title: Finance Director

Company profile
Formed in July 2001 following merger between the Book Select Service division of Nexus Publishing Group and Books Plus of W.F. Goddard. Now UK market leader in the selection, distribution, selling and marketing of books to retailers.

Employer brand
Books Plus Select is a customer-focused organisation that seeks to both anticipate customer needs and exceed expectations. Our premier position has been achieved through building long-term business partnerships with customers and suppliers alike. Our employees strive for excellence in all that they do. Staff are encouraged to think for themselves and demonstrate initiative in an atmosphere of openness. Staff have a sense of belonging in an environment which is supportive, committed and fun. Our selection process is designed to be an open, collaborative joint venture.

Primary function
As a key member of the senior management team, the finance director contributes actively to the strategic direction of the company and works closely with the managing director on the development of the business. The finance director controls and directs the finance, administration and IT activities of the company.

Reports to
Managing director.

Supervising authority over
Accounts, IT and administration functions, comprising 32 staff.

Direct reports
Financial accountant, credit controller, management accountant, director of IT.

Responsibilities
1. Responsible for the finance and IT functions and formulation of forward strategy.
2. Reviewing monthly management reporting package and preparing detailed finance report.
3. Co-ordinating and reviewing quarterly forecasts, annual budget and three-year plan.
4. Setting cash flow targets for credit control and ensuring cash balances are maximised.
5. Directing the continued development of sound financial controls and systems.
6. Advising managing director on all aspects of finance.
7. Contributing towards the development of the business as part of the senior management team.
8. Ensuring group and company policies are adhered to.
9. Reviewing capital spend proposals.
10. Directing the development of computer-based systems.

Figure 7.1

A word of warning when drafting the job description: it is not sufficient simply to rummage through old files and pull out the job description that was used when recruiting for the position last time round. The precise role now needing to be filled will almost certainly have changed in some, if not all, respects. Consider the technology and processes being used now compared to three years ago.

If in doubt about the role, call on the help of those most closely involved with it – namely the present incumbent and his or her colleagues. If someone has resigned from the role, one of their final tasks before leaving could be to produce a detailed outline of how they see the role. What exactly do they do each day? Who are the key individuals they work with? What are the key challenges involved in the role? What have they found most rewarding?

Although line managers, or HR departments, may think they have a reasonable idea about what is involved in a particular role, even the most conscientious and involved managers will struggle to know exactly what every member of the team does all the time. So make the most of the expert – the incumbent – and tap their knowledge and insights before they walk out of the door for the last time.

The next step is to define what the organisation needs in terms of the type of person who will be able to fill the job description. This means drawing up a candidate profile.

The candidate profile

Required: superhuman multitalented brain box. This may be the ideal candidate for the role, but the first rule when drawing up the candidate profile is to keep a grip on reality. This means distinguishing between 'must haves' and 'nice to haves' in the skills, experience and competencies required.

A typical candidate profile would include:

- qualifications;
- practical experience;
- personality traits/competencies;
- career aspirations.

Qualifications
Does the role require a university graduate? Are additional professional qualifications required to indicate that the individual has the appropriate depth of knowledge or technical ability?

Practical experience
How much similarity is required between the candidate's current or recent role and the job description? The specified experience should indicate what level of seniority suitable applicants should have had when gaining their experience, as well as the type and extent of that experience.

Personality traits/competencies
Research by Stanford University indicates that around 80% of career success is determined by competency in terms of people's behaviour. Someone may have skills and qualifications coming out of their ears, but if they do not have the necessary behavioural competencies appropriate to the job in question, then those skills and qualifications will be undermined.

Issues to consider include:

- Is this a customer-facing role requiring attributes such as patience and strong verbal communication ability?
- Is this a back-room role where interpersonal skills are less important than the ability to work well unsupervised?
- Will the successful candidate need to be able to motivate a team, and therefore need proven leadership ability?
- Does the role need someone with the drive and resourcefulness to go out and drum up business, someone with enough of a tough skin to be able to cope with repeated knock-backs?
- Will the role require counselling skills, where the individual will need to be a good listener, able to offer guidance without dominating those seeking help?

Career aspirations
It may be that the recruiting organisation seeks someone with high ambitions, someone who will see the role as providing an opportunity to develop new skills and then progress rapidly up through the ranks. Alternatively, perhaps someone who wants a period of stability may fit better into the team, which has itself undergone a series of changes and now requires a period of time to settle down.

By considering the preferred aspirations of the successful candidate, the recruiting organisation is less likely to make mistakes such as 'over-recruiting' – bringing in someone with high expectations who will be frustrated by the actual role on offer.

In Figure 7.2, we have developed a fictional candidate profile for Books Plus Select, building on the job description developed in Figure 7.1.

BOOKS PLUS SELECT

Candidate Profile: Finance Director

Qualifications	Qualified accountant
Previous experience	Will have already held a senior finance position in a medium/ large dynamic organisation.
	Experience in fast moving consumer goods would be an advantage.
	At least five-years post qualifying experience.
	Experience of managing a large department.
	Sound knowledge of computer-based systems and preferably would have actively contributed to systems development.
Personal attributes	Must not be an 'ivory tower'. Must be prepared to lead by example.
	Commercial approach. Must be capable of and prepared to contribute to the development of the business by constantly searching for opportunities to improve the business.
	Mobile. Must be prepared to travel between Northants and Surrey.
	Communication. Ability to influence and energise others by communicating a clear and attractive growth vision.
	Change catalyst. Capable of promoting and endorsing organisational change efforts.
	People development. Actively developing others, providing frequent coaching and feedback.
	Empowering others. Delegating to others to allow them to take the lead and create shared responsibility. Creating space for initiative and innovation.
Aspirations	Seeks a senior finance role with a significant IT component and the opportunity to make a commercial contribution. Does not aspire to a general management position in the short/medium term.

Figure 7.2

Managing the recruitment process

Once the job description and candidate profile have been drafted, the organisation needs to consider precisely how it intends to go about finding the desired new recruit.

Specific issues to consider include:

- Can the recruitment be managed totally in-house, or does the organisation need to appoint a recruitment consultancy? This question is considered in detail in Chapter 8: Calling in the Cavalry: Recruitment Consultancies.
- How many potential candidates might exist in the market-place? This will impact on the recruitment method. For example, if there are likely to be plenty of potential applicants, a selection process based around an advertising campaign may be an appropriate recruitment strategy.
- If an advertising campaign is to form part of the strategy, what input can the organisation's marketing team provide to the process? Have there been any recently successful advertising campaigns which the HR team can build on when devising the recruitment advertising campaign? We look at the recruitment advertising process in Chapter 9: Effective Advertising.
- Should candidates be asked to complete a standard application form in order to compare their skills against the job description effectively, or will reviewing CVs be sufficient? We consider some of the associated pros and cons in Chapter 10: CVs and Application Forms.
- How many interviews are candidates going to attend, and with whom? If an external consultancy is appointed, it will handle the first round. But second and any further interviews will need to be conducted by HR and/or by the appropriate line manager. Are these people appropriately trained to conduct interviews effectively? The importance of interview technique – for interviewers – is highlighted in Chapter 11: Interviewing: Technique Tips and Chapter 12: Interviewing: Effective Questioning.
- Will candidates need to complete skill and aptitude tests or personality questionnaires? These results can provide valuable additional information on applicants, as we consider in Chapter 13: Testing Times.

- Who will have ultimate responsibility for the final appointment decision? How much influence will others involved in the process have? We consider how to handle the decision process in Chapter 14: The Final Selection.

Job fairs

Depending on the position needing to be filled, the recruiting organisation may want to consider whether events such as job fairs could prove useful sources of talent. Job fairs can be a useful way for employers to get out and meet potential future employees, particularly when recruiting for multiple positions at junior or mid-manager level.

Making the best use of job fairs requires extra up-front planning. For example, if the headcount budget indicates that there will be a need for new recruits in April, attending a job fair in January or February would fit well with the recruitment timescale, but doing so in March will probably be too late. The organisation's stand will need to be manned by people who represent the employer's desired brand image effectively and who can talk persuasively about opportunities there. It is a mistake to send people who are too junior or who are inadequately informed about the organisation's HR plans and recruitment processes. You also need to have plenty of literature ready to distribute and an efficient means of capturing the contact details of potentially suitable employees.

Whatever the precise recruitment process chosen, recruiters should bear in mind that their chances of success will be greatly enhanced if they concentrate on

- maximising the 'pull' factors, that is, strong employer branding;
- selecting the right selectors;
- encouraging openness;
- maintaining momentum.

Maximising the pull factors

Recruitment is not just about choosing between ranks of willing applicants. In the war for talent recruiters need to make sure they maximise their attractiveness. All organisations seeking to recruit new employees must focus on the 'pull' factors that will make a preferred candidate decide to accept a job offer.

Factors that count in the attraction game include:

- the efficiency with which applications are handled;
- the courtesy, professionalism and politeness with which candidates, even obviously unsuitable ones, are handled;
- the attractiveness of the public face shown to applicants in terms of the people they meet, whether during interviews, completing assessments or talking informally with their potential colleagues – in short, selecting the right selectors (see below);
- the openness applied to the recruitment process (see below);
- the obvious attention paid to the recruitment process, whether by proper preparation by interviewers or in the willingness to accommodate candidates by meeting them at convenient times;
- the strength and appeal of the employer brand, as discussed in Chapter 3: Strategies for Successful Recruitment;
- the consistency of the recruitment message with the external brand image, as discussed in Chapter 9: Effective Advertising.

Selecting the right selectors

The HR team must pay particular attention to making sure that the people involved in the recruitment process will have a positive impact on potential recruits. Most importantly, what impression will the interviewers make on candidates?

Research shows that as far as candidates are concerned, the interviewer becomes the personification of the organisation. If the interviewer is unprepared and disorganised, the organisation will be perceived as poorly managed. If the interviewer is chatty and open, the candidate will interpret that as meaning that the organisation is a friendly and open place in which to work. If the interviewer appears to have achieved much at an early age, the candidate will presume that the organisation seeks out and rewards talent.

This means that those handling interviews need to be considered representative of the organisation and its future direction. Avoid simply rolling out a long-server who has more in common with the organisation's culture of 10 years ago. It is worth putting in some effort to identify an interviewer likely to inspire candidates. At the very least, the importance of making a good impression must be highlighted to all those likely to have candidate contact along the way.

Encouraging openness

Modern recruits really wants to know what an organisation is like before they join. An organisation that appears open, that makes an effort to help candidates assess the culture, will create a more positive impression. Ideally, the candidate should feel that the recruitment process is a joint exploration, enabling both parties to find out about each other and reach an informed decision as to whether there is likely to be a good fit.

Openness can be demonstrated by an organisation being willing to offer feedback to unsuccessful candidates, whether following on from the completion of assessment tests or interviews. Candidates may often want to know why they have been unsuccessful, but are generally given little information. Making the offer of feedback on performance, even if such an offer is not taken up, will leave a positive impression that can only reinforce the organisation's reputation as a worthy employer.

Openness in the recruitment process can also be encouraged by including a meeting between a final-stage candidate and a potential colleague or peer. Such meetings can be held on an informal basis, on or off-site, and on the understanding that the candidate will have the opportunity to ask probing questions about what working life in the organisation is really like. 'Forget the hype, how late does everyone really stay during the week? How flexible is the training department in responding to individual needs? Why are there so few women on the team? Why did the last incumbent really leave?'

It goes without saying that the peer must be someone respected within the organisation, who is likely to create a positive impression. However, they should be given carte blanche to answer any questions put to them. They should offer their own, honest opinion. The peer's role is *not* to act as an official spin doctor, putting a fake glossy sheen on all aspects of the organisation

79

and the work. Anyone who tries this will inevitably come over as false, and will almost certainly put the candidate off. If the candidate feels he or she is not receiving reliable answers to their questions, then the whole point of the peer interview is destroyed.

Honest and open responses are also valuable for helping to set the candidate's expectations of what working life is like in the organisation. Not only does this ensure that any decision to accept a forthcoming job offer is made in a well-informed way; it also reduces the chances of someone joining with too high expectations, subsequently becoming disillusioned, losing interest in their work, performing poorly and leaving again in a relatively short time.

In general, the peer should not be expected to play an assessment role. In other words, the peer is not a member of the selection team and should not be expected to feed back an opinion as to whether this is the right candidate for the job. However, should the candidate appear overly preoccupied with any particular issues, say with the ability to leave the office on the dot each day, the peer should be able to inform the relevant line manager or HR department. They can then make a decision as to whether further formal discussion on the matter is needed with the candidate in question.

Giving candidates the chance to talk freely with someone from their potential peer group, preferably someone of a similar age and outlook, can have a dramatic impact on the rate at which job offers are converted into acceptances. One major UK retailer found that its acceptance ratio increased by around 30% as a result.

Maintaining momentum

It is important to maintain momentum throughout the recruitment process; too often organisations let things drag on.

The recruitment process should be imagined as a funnel – applicants piling in at the top, being efficiently filtered and the final choice emerging promptly at the bottom. Instead, recruitment often seems to take an unstructured linear form, with an indeterminate end date.

The following scenario is a familiar one to recruitment consultants. The recruiting organisation briefs three recruitment consultancies. Over the next few days and weeks, the consultancies send through shortlists of recommended candidates for the client to interview. These interviews progress on a haphazard basis, with the client comparing candidate with candidate, gradually losing sight of the job description and pre-agreed candidate profile. The decision-making process starts to stretch...

During this process, recruitment consultants become familiar with conversations such as this:

Jeff: 'Hi there, Rob. I'm just phoning to see what you thought of those last candidates we referred to you. They had some impressive experience between them, don't you think?'

Rob: 'Jeff, yes indeed. I was quite impressed, but ...'

Jeff: 'Is there a problem?'

Rob: 'Well, I really liked what Kate had to offer, but then I thought maybe she wouldn't get on too well with some of the other team members. John was also good, and clearly also meets our needs, but I was really hoping for someone with a little more charisma. So I'm not sure what to say. Any chance you could keep both of those two warm for me? Perhaps I should just see a few more people ...'

Now, here is a question: how are recruitment consultants supposed to keep candidates warm? Are their offices filled with rows of incubators? No! Keeping candidates warm is extremely difficult. Employers who leave people hanging on without giving them either an offer, a rejection or a call-back for a further meeting run the risk of losing that candidate's interest.

This is bad practice for several reasons. First, real talent does not hang around. If you think you have found someone suitable for the position in question, who has the right competencies, snap them up. Secondly, leaving a candidate dangling will create a bad impression. Do the recruiters really know what they are doing? How good can they really be on the international arena if they cannot manage to make up their minds quickly about one single job?

The most successful recruitment campaigns are highly structured, with a timetable planned from start to finish. For example, if using an advertising campaign, the date of the advertisements are known. Within perhaps two weeks of the final advertisement the recruitment consultancy will provide a shortlist of candidates for the organisation to interview. Second round interviews can be scheduled for the period up to 10 days after that with any testing occurring around the same time. A decision will be taken in the following week.

This means that candidates can be given a relatively precise indication of how the recruitment process will proceed and when they are likely to know the recruiter's decision. The recruiting organisation can also make assumptions about likely start dates, assuming that candidates may be on one month or three months notice, depending on seniority. If temporary cover is likely to be needed in the meantime, plans for that can also get underway.

Working through the recruitment process against such a time-table will ensure that momentum is maintained – good news for recruiting organisations and candidates alike.

Public sector issues

In recent times, there has been an increasing crossover between public and private sector activities. Government initiatives to encourage private involvement in formerly public sector areas have encouraged a cross-fertilisation of business practices between the two.

However, in recruitment there remain some distinct differences in the ways that private and public sector organisations operate. We comment on some of the issues as they affect public sector recruiters in the appropriate sections; here, we highlight some general key differences.

Common key characteristics of the public sector recruitment process include:

- advertising almost all positions;
- producing information packs for candidates;
- using application forms rather than relying on CVs;
- holding panel interviews rather that one-to-ones;
- emphasising equal opportunities.

The private sector could perhaps learn from certain public sector practices, particularly the extent of information given to applicants and the focus on equal opportunity.

Advertising

Public sector organisations may well use a combination of search (head-hunting) and selection following an advertising campaign, but very few positions are filled by means of a search process only. The advertised selection approach fits in with the predominant public sector philosophy of encouraging open and fair competition.

However, recruitment advertising is a skilful business. In Chapter 9: Effective Advertising, we look at some of the errors to which public sector organisations can be particularly prone.

Information packs

Most public sector recruiters still expect candidates who respond to an advertised vacancy to contact the recruiter (by phone or e-mail) by a specified date to request an information pack. This pack will contain a wealth of information on the vacant position and the organisation itself. Typical contents include:

- a job specification;
- a candidate profile or specification;
- an organisation chart;
- a copy of the annual report;
- the organisation's mission or vision statement;
- a letter from the individual to whom the applicant would report in the role;
- details of pay and benefits;
- employment policies (including equal opportunities);
- an application form (and monitoring form);
- instructions for how to respond.

If public sector organisations are to do this, they must pay attention to preparing an impressive pack. 'The general standard of information packs is terrible, but branding and reputation management is critical,' says Hamish Davidson, Head of the UK Executive Search and Selection Division at Pricewaterhouse-Coopers, and a public sector specialist. 'What's the point of paying out for an advert claiming to be a 21st century organisation and sending out an awful briefing pack? You have to give some thought to the fact that you need to entice people in. You need to make sure the documentation sells the position.'

The style of the material needs to be as professional as the content: scrappy photocopies will not impress. The information also needs to be honest and realistic. There is no point claiming to be a top-performing organisation if there has been extensive recent press coverage highlighting internal or performance problems. Unsupportable claims will be met with candidate cynicism.

Application forms

Application forms have a strong historical tradition in public sector recruiting. They were initially introduced primarily for the recruitment of staff at lower levels, people not necessarily familiar with having to prepare CVs, but their use spread to more senior levels as well. In a culture where creating equal opportunities was seen as an important goal, forms seemed to fit the bill: they could be tailored to focus on key competencies for the job in question and candidates could then be initially selected for interview on the basis of their evidential suitability, in relation to the desired competencies, as shown in their completed forms.

In Chapter 10: CVs and Application Forms, we look at the advantages and disadvantages of application forms in recruitment, and how to use them effectively when selecting candidates for interview.

Panel interviews

Selection decisions in most public sector organisations are generally made by an appointments panel or selection committee. Appointments panels are designed to rule out any one person's potential bias determining the decision. They are intended as part of a due process to ensure that an equal opportunity is given to each candidate to impress.

The use of appointments panels in the public sector inevitably means that candidates undergo panel interviews, and panel interviews are certainly more common in the public than the private sector.

This can mean that perhaps as many as 20 people are involved in the interview session although wherever possible, such large numbers should be avoided because of the extra difficulty involved in organising such a group. We consider issues of panel size, as well as some of the advantages and disadvantages of panel interviews, in Chapter 11: Interviewing: Technique Tips.

Equal opportunity and diversity

Concern to achieve equal opportunity in the recruitment process is particularly notable in the public sector, where most obvious effort is made to avoid discriminating against people by reason of race, gender, age, disability or religion.

Overt discrimination is easy to spot; but covert discrimination can be tougher to avoid. This means that when planning the recruitment process, specific thought needs to be given to each element to ensure that no unconscious discrimination is coming into play. We consider some of the issues involved in Chapter 9: Effective Advertising, Chapter 10: CVs and Application Forms and Chapter 13: Testing Times.

Attracting private sector applicants

The increasing cross-fertilisation between public and private sectors means that more public sector organisations are attracting applications from people with careers founded in private sector practices. This is good news, since the exchanging of best practice between both sectors should help to improve the operation of both. However, public sector recruiters may need to adjust some of their recruitment ways if they are to maximise their private sector appeal. They could do this by:

Reducing rigidity
Public sector recruiters may need to soften some of their more rigid recruiting habits, if they are to succeed in persuading private sector talent to join them. For example, individuals with a track record of working in the private sector are more likely to be put off by having to complete an application form, rather than being able to send in their CV.

Explaining the process more thoroughly
Private sector applicants may also require a more detailed explanation of the recruitment process up-front, including the way that the appointments panel will reach its decision.

If the organisation's policy is to offer the job to their preferred candidate after the final panel interview, then applicants should be told of this likelihood; in the private sector offers are not normally made on the spot, and so candidates may not be expecting to have to make up their minds there and then.

Actively attracting

Too often public sector recruiters forget that selection is only part of the recruitment process; attraction is another vital element required for success. For example, the fact that some public sector organisations will offer the job to a candidate immediately after the final panel interview suggests they assume that all candidates will automatically want to take the job if offered it, without needing any time for further consideration. This is despite the fact that the final interview may have identified issues that the candidate might want to consider quietly later, or talk over with a partner.

Organisations should ensure they have given the candidate sufficient information on which to make an informed decision. For example, it is good practice to ensure that short-listed candidates have a briefing meeting, not an interview as such, with the individual who would be their direct boss. This person will be involved in any panel interview, but a one-to-one meeting is essential if the candidate is to be able to assess whether the two can work together. This sounds like obvious common sense, but it does not always happen in the public sector.

An assumption that the preferred candidate will accept the offer can be a symptom of a general lack of awareness of the need to consider applicants' needs and concerns. These needs should be considered when planning the recruitment process. For example, if panel interviews are being held, then panel members may prefer to see short-listed candidates one after the other. However, applicants holding senior posts elsewhere may not be able to fit easily into a certain time slot on a particular day. They may need more flexibility, or the guarantee of an early morning or after hours interview.

Similarly, when filling senior posts, recruiters should be sensitive to candidates' desire for confidentiality; top people are unlikely to want to be bumping into their rival candidates in a conveyor-belt interview period. In one case, an organisation's attempts to maintain confidentiality by spacing out candidates' interviews during a day's selection session were scuppered when a list of names was left lying prominently at reception.

The same reasons of diary conflicts and desire for confidentiality can also cause problems for public sector organisations that want to hold group assessments, or who require short-listed applicants to attend an evening dinner, the night before a final selection day. It might seem appealing to have rival candidates swapping seats round the room with each course, but more senior applicants may prefer to withdraw their application rather than take part.

Sometimes appointments panel members may simply forget that lack of common courtesy, such as failing to welcome interviewees properly, will create a bad impression on candidates. It is not unknown for recruitment consultants to find themselves apologising to candidates for the rudeness of their client organisations.

Above all, public sector recruiters must not forget that they have to sell the vacancy they are trying to fill. Why would this interest a talented person? What are the challenges? Pay and benefits are unlikely to be the main rewards, so what are the key attractions of the position?

If the organisation needs advice on these issues, a quality recruitment consultancy should be able to help. When planning your recruitment process, one of the early decisions to be taken concerns whether or not to use recruitment consultants. We consider issues involved in the decision, and how to use recruitment consultancies effectively, in the next chapter.

Chapter 8

Calling in the Cavalry: Recruitment Consultancies

Recruitment is a priority activity for any successful business. So when a recruitment need arises, the organisation has to consider whether it has the resources (in terms of skills and personnel time) to manage that process effectively. If it does not, that means bringing in external specialist help.

Can you handle recruitment in-house?

Considering the following questions can help identify whether sufficient in-house resources exist:

- Do you have a dedicated HR individual who can take responsibility for drawing up the job and candidate specification?
- Does this person have the necessary expertise to understand the particular, current issues in that sector of the job market, at the specific seniority level?
- Can the position be filled by means of a selection process based around a job advertisement?
- Do you have the resources to be able to spend time sifting through CVs to select first-round interview candidates?
- Do you have the flexibility to be able to interview those candidates early in the morning, later in the evening or generally at times that suit them?

If the answers to all the above are affirmative, then conducting the recruitment in-house is a viable possibility.

However, if there are some definite 'Nos', then it may be worth bringing in an external recruitment consultant.

Reasons for appointing a recruitment consultancy

Calling in external help may be appropriate where some or all of the following conditions exist:

- lack of in-house recruitment expertise;
- lack of in-house time to handle applications;
- you are unsure what the best approach may be to attract applicants for the vacant position(s);
- the role is so high level or in such a specialised area that advertising the position is unlikely to generate a significant number of appropriate applications; or
- you need guidance on current market demand and pay rates for the type of individual required.

Apart from overcoming these challenges, there may be additional benefits from appointing a recruitment consultancy. For example, research suggests that senior candidates prefer dealing with an intermediary when making an initial response to a job advertisement. This is because once an advertisement has sparked some curiosity, potential applicants still want to know a little more about the details of the position before spending time and effort tailoring their CV or filling in an application form. Therefore, they like having the option of being able to phone the named recruitment consultancy and have an informal discussion about the vacancy, checking particular details that may be key to their decision whether to apply or not.

The recruitment consultancy can act as an unpaid adviser to potential applicants, giving them an indication of whether they may have the skills and experience desired by the recruiting organisation. If a candidate appears to lack key requirements, the consultancy can stop them wasting their own and everyone else's time. But if a candidate seems to fit the bill, the consultancy's enthusiasm may encourage them to go ahead with an application. The consultancy can generally help to keep communication channels open with candidates, and ensure that momentum is maintained throughout the recruitment process.

If external help is needed, the next step is to decide which type of recruitment firm will be most appropriate for the current need.

Head-hunters, selection consultancies and recruitment consultancies/agencies

There are many different types of recruitment firms in the marketplace offering their services. Unfortunately, they do not all do the same things.

Traditionally the recruitment marketplace could be characterised as containing clearly distinct types of firms, ranging from head-hunters at the top end, to agencies at the bottom. The services they offered were quite distinct:

- Head-hunters, more formally known as 'executive search' firms, were appointed to handle the most senior, or most specific, assignments. Head-hunters never placed advertisements to drum up interest from candidates, but focused on search activity. This meant they used their sector knowledge, backed up by research, to track down potential candidates and headhunt them.
- Selection consultancies handled assignments where advertising the vacancy was expected to attract a sufficient number of qualified applicants. They would sift through the CVs received in response, interview an initial selection and put forward a short-list of suitable candidates to the client for second round interviews. These firms would also offer a degree of advice to their clients on how to recruit the likely candidate successfully, thus justifying the description of their services as 'consultancy'.
- Recruitment consultancies/agencies primarily tried to identify likely candidates from their existing databases of job seekers, perhaps running general advertisements to attract new applicants.

Over the years the distinctions between these different types of firms have blurred. Head-hunters may consider advertising a vacancy as well as conducting a search, while selection consultancies will offer headhunting services for senior appointments instead of, or in addition to, their advertising-driven work. Many 'search and selection' firms also maintain databases containing details of individuals who have responded to past advertising campaigns. Some recruitment agencies will also take a more proactive approach and advertise vacancies as well as occasionally conducting some limited search activity.

In one sense, this blurring of services makes life easier for client organisations, since you can obtain a bundle of different services from a single supplier. However, when appointing a recruitment firm to handle an assignment it will be necessary to clarify exactly what type of services they provide, whether any particular aspect is their speciality and how successful they tend to be in using different methods.

Choosing the right approach

Consultancies should be able to offer advice on the recruitment approach that will best suit the client's particular needs. For example, there is no point advertising if the people being targeted are known not to look for job moves in that way, or if the desired skills are highly specialised. If there are believed to be only six people in the country with the appropriate knowledge of human genome theory, then advertising will be a waste of money. On the other hand, candidates for some junior roles may not spend much time reading job advertisements but instead simply sign on with a number of recruitment agencies. In such cases, there may be little added benefit from advertising or conducting a search since a recruitment agency may be able to draw up a suitable list of potential candidates almost immediately.

However, do not just take advice without considering whether it really makes sense. Some search specialists may argue that the position should be filled by means of search alone, when advertising could usefully smoke out a few extra candidates that the consultancy's researchers could otherwise overlook. If you really believe there is a case for advertising as well, it is probably worth paying the extra cost.

In general, a sensible approach is to expect that the most senior roles will need a headhunting activity, upper middle roles may require a combination of search and selection, while a local agency may be able to fill junior roles by a simple database search, backed up by selection if necessary. Specialist consultancies/agencies may be best when seeking to fill specialist roles, such as in IT, accounting or law.

The typical process

In whatever way that the recruitment consultancy identifies potential candidates, whether via a database run, an advertised selection process or by headhunting, it will provide an initial screening service for clients. Consultancies will interview first-round candidates to whittle them down to a short-list. In a selection-based assignment, the consultancy might interview around 12 people, before putting forward between three and five short listed candidates. With a search assignment, consultancies may interview slightly fewer individuals up-front. This is because the research involved in the headhunting process requires the consultant to speak to past or present colleagues or bosses when identifying potential candidates. This means that the consultant should already have extensive knowledge about the person before they even come for an interview. However, with a selection process, all the consultant may have to work with is the applicant's CV, so that more people may need to be interviewed in order to get a true perspective of who the best candidates are.

Selecting the consultancy

The recruiting organisation may already have identified a number of appropriate recruitment firms for use in particular situations. If not, then some time needs to be spent identifying which from the target group will be most likely to meet your needs.

'It is a bit like a patient choosing the surgeon; you want to make sure they have performed the operation before.' So says Suzzane Wood, Partner and Head of the Financial Management Practice at executive search consultants Odgers Ray & Berndtson.

Do not overlook these basic selection criteria:

- Look for a firm with appropriate sectoral and even functional specialism. For example, within the accountancy sector, one firm may have extensive experience of recruiting tax and treasury personnel, but little track record in internal audit or management accounting.
- Check that the firm has recruitment experience at the appropriate seniority level. A consultancy may promote itself as

expert in recruiting for positions paying salary packages from £20,000 to £120,000. But how many do they really recruit at that top level? It could be one person every six months, while the majority of their recruitment activity occurs at the £40,000 to £60,000 level. Ask for specific examples of successful assignments similar to your own.

- Does the consultancy's style and approach fit your organisation's culture? The recruitment consultancy will be acting as an ambassador for your organisation, having the initial contact with applicants. First impressions count, so you need to be confident they will be the right ones.

Once you have made some initial enquiries and identified a couple of likely consultancies that appear to meet the above criteria, hold a 'beauty parade'. Make sure that the people who come to see you will be the people who will actually handle your assignment. A consultancy may send along an impressive presenter who knows all about your sector and who appears to understand your needs exactly, but once the firm is appointed, you may never see this individual again.

Chris Long, partner in senior executive search consultancy Whitehead Mann, says: 'Running a successful search assignment requires the search organisation not only to be able to represent the client organisation in the best possible light, but also to develop a relationship with quality candidates. Top quality people are usually getting approached quite frequently. Therefore, you have to differentiate your approach. There is nothing worse than a poorly prepared approach from a search organisation that lets the client down. It comes down to the calibre of the consultant handling the assignment. The best head-hunters are the ones who are prepared to go the extra mile in managing the rigours of the process and in building a strong relationship with the preferred candidate, even helping them through the process of resignation from their current employer. It is that kind of attention to detail that the client should be paying for.'

Off-limits restrictions

When appointing a head-hunter to perform a senior level search, make sure you ask which companies or organisations are 'off-limits'. Firms enter into off-limits agreements for a variety of reasons, perhaps because they do a significant amount of work for the organisation, or because they assist with extremely senior appointments. In this case, the client organisation will want to make sure that the information the head-hunter learns will remain confidential.

However, 'off limits' agreements can vary, so as well as finding out which organisations are covered, ask about the terms of the agreement as well. Recruitment consultancies should be open about these policies, but you must ask. Otherwise you run the risk that in three months' time the search is floundering but the most obvious candidate in a rival organisation has not been approached because the head-hunter simply cannot do so.

Suzzane Wood recommends asking for contactable client references. She says: 'Very few organisations actually do that. Ideally you should ask to speak to someone the consultancy has just worked with on a recent assignment. Ring them up and ask informally how it went.'

Success rates

Do not forget to ask what the consultancy's success rates are using different strategic approaches. Across the industry a search assignment generally has a 75% success rate, while selection assignments should have a somewhat higher hit rate. This is simply due to the fact that even if a head-hunter finds the perfect individual for a client's needs, that individual may have no intention of leaving his or her existing employer. Even the most brilliant search consultant cannot *make* someone want to move jobs. However, anyone who responds to an advertised vacancy has already indicated their readiness to change roles, so the consultant's persuasive task is vastly reduced.

However, as Suzzane Wood says: 'You could argue that search activity should have a higher completion rate, because it goes on until a person is found for the job. The consulting firm will continue until it has exhausted the marketplace. A consultant will never cancel an assignment unless the client changes the parameters of the search, decides to call a halt, makes an internal appointment or goes through some unexpected change like a takeover.'

When a consultancy tells you its success or completion rates, ask how they calculate them. Some may try and fudge the figures. Does its definition of 'completion' always mean that they found an appropriate individual for the specified role? If a consultancy claims an impressively high success rate, make them justify it.

Costs

The fees charged by specialist recruitment consultancies will clearly vary depending on the service provided. The more complex the assignment and the more proactive the activity required by the recruitment firm, the higher the fee.

Typical rates

For a pure search to headhunt an individual for a senior position, the generally accepted fee is equivalent to a third of the successful appointee's first year package. This will take into account base salary, any realistically expected bonus, share options and other executive benefits.

Where a consultancy supplements its full search service with an advertisement, the client will also pay the associated advertising costs. The client organisation may benefit, however, from discounts in advertising rates that the recruitment firm has been able to negotiate because of its frequent custom. This can mean that the advertising costs paid by the recruiting organisation may be half what it would have paid had it bought the same advertising space directly itself.

Where the main focus is placed on a selection strategy using advertising, with the consultancy only providing a limited search to back it up, the fee may then be calculated as perhaps one third of the first year's salary package. A limited search in this context may simply mean that the consultancy targets potential candidates in an agreed number of likely organisations, rather than undertaking to conduct an open-ended search until the assignment is completed.

For junior positions, if no search activity is required, the fee may be perhaps 20–25% of the successful candidate's pay and benefits package. The cost for a relatively junior role paying £25,000 would be around the £5,000 mark.

Rather than agreeing to a fee which will vary depending on the successful appointee's pay and benefits, some organisations prefer to negotiate an agreed, fixed fee up-front. Consultancies should be open to this approach, although the consultancy's negotiations will still be shaped by the expected total value of the salary package on offer for the vacant role.

Value for money?

The recruitment consultancies' fees may appear steep on first sight. Successfully finding a chief executive on a package of £500,000 could cost £165,000. However, a consultancy that does its job well can save its clients the costs associated with making mistakes both in the recruitment process applied and in the final appointment. For example, consultancies can prevent clients pouring money down the drain by placing an expensive and pointless advertisement in the wrong media, which their target candidate pool is known to ignore.

Furthermore, it is generally accepted that the cost of recruiting the wrong person is equivalent to twice that person's salary. This recruiting maxim takes into account the disruption caused by management downtime, lowered morale, repeat recruitment fees, adverse publicity, negative impact on customers or clients and so on. Against this background, the fees charged by recruitment consultancies appear rather reasonable.

Preferred supplier agreements

Some organisations try to negotiate lower, discounted fees in return for a preferred supplier arrangement. Do not be tempted to do the same. If a consultancy feels it is receiving inadequate compensation for its services, the chances are it will not put its best people to work on your account. The lowest cost, most junior, least experienced staff are probably what you will get. If you are trying to recruit senior level posts you could find you have made a very false economy.

However, a preferred supplier agreement may provide added value where the fees are unaffected but where the recruitment consultancy is given the chance to build a long-term relationship with your organisation. Suzzane Wood explains: 'An organisation may say it is thinking of giving us all their business, and wants to discuss the service we will provide. We can then talk about coming to see them every week, building a deep knowledge of their business, helping them with organisational issues and so on. These are some of the value-added services that you can get from a preferred supplier agreement.'

Getting the best service

Even without opting for a preferred supplier agreement, you want to make sure you get the best service possible from your appointed recruitment consultancy. This means choosing a firm with which you feel you can develop a strong business relationship.

Close co-operation

Some organisations seem to want to keep their appointed recruitment consultancies at arm's length. Perhaps this is because the in-house HR team consider the external advisers to be rivals in some way, or feel at a disadvantage because the consultancy firm has more specialist knowledge about recruitment. Unfortunately, keeping your distance from the external recruitment consultants can limit the ultimate success of the search process.

The recruitment process involves a triangular connection between the in-house HR team, the line manager with the talent need, and the external recruitment consultant. All parties have the same goal – a successful appointment – and all stand to gain from achieving that goal: the HR team and the line manager appoints the talent it needs to take its business forward, and the consultancy earns its fee and has the satisfaction of a job well done.

Suzzane Wood says: 'Organisations need to think of us as a business partner, not just as a supplier. If you think of a search firm just as a supplier, it will never work, you will never get value for money. The search firm must be treated as a trusted business partner. We can help in the business in more ways than simply finding the right person for a vacancy. The information that we gather in the course of an assignment can be very valuable. We can inform clients on market trends, salary and package information, what people are saying about the organisation – how they are perceived, and what people are saying about competitors as well. It is true consultancy work and a search firm will regard itself as equal to your lawyers, bankers, and management consultants.'

Some recruitment consultancies may ask to speak to the line manager who originally flagged up the role to be filled. Some HR departments will refuse such requests as being unnecessary, insisting that they are able to provide all the information the consultant should need. However, such requests should not automatically be brushed aside. It may be that the recruitment consultant wishes to pick up on the particular nuances associated with that particular role in that particular team in that specific organisation; even HR may not understand these nuances in depth. While there is no point bothering line managers with trivial questions, allowing the consultancy to speak with the line managers at the coal face can be useful where the consultancy makes a reasonable case for that dialogue. Direct contact can enable the consultant to pick up on some of the emotional, gut-feel factors that will differentiate the candidate who would do from the candidate who would fit the team like a glove.

Chris Long says: 'Good head-hunters work as an extension of the client organisation so that they are well-briefed. The best quality headhunting usually happens with clients where there is openness, honesty and respect on both sides. That helps us to target the right sort of individual for that organisation. The values and culture fit between an individual and the organisation are every bit as important as the person's achievement record and management competencies. No matter how talented the individual, if you don't get the culture fit right, it can lead to a sub-optimal solution. So success depends on knowing your client well.'

Referencing services

One key area where head-hunters can add value to the search for a senior candidate is in the taking of references. Chris Long says: 'Speaking as an ex-international HR director, this is an area which is often undervalued by clients – the process of making sure the consultant talks to the referees, can frame the key challenges of the role and drills down into the areas that are most relevant to it.'

When using a head-hunter, reference taking to some extent happens at two levels. Initially, when consultants are at the sourcing stage, they speak to people in the industry to identify potentially suitable candidates. This process involves talking in fairly general terms about why certain people are respected and recommended. Then later, as the recruitment process is moving closer to the offer stage, the time comes for more formal references to be followed up. At this point consultants need to be sensitive to the candidate's position, particularly if no formal job offer has yet been made; the candidate will not want their current employer to hear word of their potential move on the grapevine. This is a particular danger when taking references from past employers.

However, head-hunters can be particularly valuable during this formal reference taking stage. Chris Long says: 'We are experienced in asking the right questions. We may also be able to be a bit more direct and challenging. Head-hunters can be particularly useful when someone has lost one of their stars to a rival organisation; if that organisation then phones up for a reference, the terms of engagement can be far from smooth sailing. If a head-hunter phones up for the reference, it may make things a little easier for the referee to distance themselves from the situation.'

Control and monitoring

Once a recruitment consultancy is appointed for an executive level appointment, it should provide a written proposal confirming its understanding of the client's needs. The document should include:

- the consultancy's understanding of the assignment, including the role to be filled;
- an indication of the consultancy's depth of understanding of the marketplace;
- an outline approach for completing the assignment;

- the likely timescale involved;
- an indication of target organisations where the successful candidate may be found;
- an indication of how much potential candidates are likely to be earning;
- the expected salary package the recruiting organisation may have to offer;
- the basis for the consultancy's fees; and
- details of the consultancy's staff who will be working on the assignment.

As the assignment proceeds, the in-house HR team needs to maintain regular contact with the consultancy, gaining progress reports and any revised opinions on how long the process is likely to take. As the consultancy starts to generate a short-list of candidates for interview, the recruiting organisation needs to give precise feedback on why some candidates are considered unsuitable, while others are favoured. Maintaining such two-way information gives the recruitment process the maximum chance of success in the minimum possible timeframe.

Recruiting organisations who do not give feedback and who persist in keeping consultancies at arms length should not be surprised if they ultimately pay a high fee for a shoddy service. Without clear instructions, the recruitment agency will be searching in the dark.

Whether or not you decide to use a recruitment consultancy, you may well want to advertise your vacancy to attract applications. We consider how to go about this effectively in the next chapter.

Chapter 9

Effective Advertising

A dvertising job vacancies is not only a traditional method of attracting applications from suitable job-hunters; it is also a way of promoting the employer's image in the wider marketplace. Job advertising is therefore an extremely important activity that can enhance or detract from an organisation's public reputation and potential recruitment success.

Building on the employer brand

Recruitment advertising needs to reflect and build on the employer brand. As we considered in Chapter 3: Strategies for Successful Recruitment, the employer brand encapsulates the way that current employees see their employer and the employment experience. A strong employer brand can also be used to attract applications from potential recruits.

Advertising job vacancies fulfils the purpose not just of attracting applicants, but also of reinforcing the organisation's public image. For example, if a business is opening a new office or a retailer is opening a new shop, the first public awareness of this often occurs through the advertising of the new jobs being created. Recruitment advertising therefore can have a major impact on the public's wider perception of the organisation and its employer brand.

As a result, it is not surprising that successful recruitment advertising increasingly involves a triangular approach involving the advertising agency, the HR team and the organisation's marketing team, rather than being simply the preserve of the agency and HR. This ensures a coherent message and communication style between the employer branding and other forms of corporate marketing activity.

Visual images and marketing styles do make a difference to the way that people perceive organisations and the employment opportunities they offer. Andrea Burrows, Managing Director of Recruitment Advertising and Marketing Specialists Associates in Advertising (AIA), uses the following example: 'Imagine you are walking down a country lane. The birds are singing, the sun is shining and there is a wonderful smell of freshly mown grass. You come across a handwritten sign painted on a blackboard. It says "Fresh eggs". You start imagining the hens scratching around for pieces of fresh corn and lovely brown eggs with bits of straw stuck to them. It gives you a pleasant feeling. You then walk on and come to another handwritten blackboard sign: "Flying lessons". How does that make you feel? Not so good. It's not appropriate for the audience.'

Market understanding

Before writing a job advertisement it is essential to consider and understand the motivations and aspirations of the target candidate pool. The advertisement must then reflect that understanding by demonstrating how well the role would enable these people to fulfil their career aims.

As we have said in Chapter 2: The Candidate Agenda, Generation X job seekers may be looking for some different things from their careers than preceding generations. Therefore, the advertisement must push the right buttons. If your target applicant is likely to be a member of the Generation X age group, bear in mind that they have more interest in work–life balance issues and corporate responsibility. They will be looking for employers who exhibit those characteristics and so the advertisement should try and get those messages across.

The motto of McCann-Erickson, the recruitment advertising specialist, is 'Truth well told'. Robert Peasnell, UK Managing Director of McCann-Erickson Recruitment, explains that job advertising should be about understanding the truth – what it is about the role or the recruiting organisation that is unique – and then getting that message across. He says: 'The challenge is to find those secret nuggets, a lot of which may involve speaking to people in the organisation about why they joined, why they have stayed and what motivates them. You have to find out what it is that makes this company or this role different to competitors.'

To get the best results, employers using an advertising agency to write the advertising copy must ensure they give the agency a full briefing. This should cover areas such as the culture of the organisation and the department in which the vacancy is located, and the reason for the recruitment need, as well as all the specific information about the role itself (such as job title, purpose and content of the role, candidate qualities required and salary). Above all, the employer needs to communicate clearly to the agency, and in the resulting advert, why the kind of person required would want to work there.

Andrea Burrows of AIA says: 'The most successful ads tend to be where you take a brief from someone in the line role about why they joined and what it is about the role that makes it interesting. You can't expect someone in HR to fundamentally understand what makes every person tick. So its good to have a combination of HR steering you on the kind of person it's reasonable to recruit, and the line giving you that suggestion about what made them join, or where their superstars have come from.' For example, the HR department of a breakdown recovery company might think that it is the blue-chip name that attracts applicants, when the recovery mechanics themselves will say it is primarily the up-to-date training they get on every new type of engine.

Contents of the advertisement

PricewaterhouseCoopers Executive Search and Selection conducted an extensive survey amongst UK managers in 1999, looking at Top Jobs Recruitment Advertising. Of the managers surveyed, only 19% said they only looked at recruitment advertisements when looking for a job and 51% said they read the appointments section each week. Asked what elements of an advertisement might entice them to consider a new opportunity when they were actively job hunting, 78% stated the attractiveness of the role would do so and 73% the salary, with 46% citing the location.

Recruiters who do best in attracting applications are the ones who recognise the importance of providing people with such key information. Advertisements must contain the triggers that will encourage appropriately qualified people to respond, while dissuading those who have inadequate skills or experience.

Essential contents of recruitment advertisements are:

Job title: Candidates like to get an idea of the level of the post and what is involved. The job title used in the advertisement should therefore be one readily understood by the target candidate and that best describes the job. If the recruiting organisation uses unusual job titles, that only make sense to other internal employees, the advertisement should ignore them and use a form of words that will be widely understood.

Salary: Experience shows that leaving any indication of salary out of an advertisement reduces the number of applications received. Research by Robert Half International found that 64% of candidates were put off responding to an advertisement that omitted the salary. Job seekers use the salary indication as a means of assessing whether the job is appropriate for them. The salary information is as much a positive filter as a negative one. Even if an advertisement says that the job offers an 'excellent salary', job-hunters will actually assume that it is not very good. Similarly, applicants interpret 'competitive salary' to mean that it is a poorly paid job. The only real justification for omitting the salary would be because of some internal sensitivities.

Location: Job seekers like to know where the recruiting organisation is based. Robert Half International's research found that 81% of candidates would not respond to an advertisement without a location. Omitting the location, or putting some vague description such as 'based in the South East of England' may make potential candidates suspicious, on the grounds that there must be something wrong with the location if the employer will not reveal it. It may be possible to influence applicants' perceptions of a location by highlighting its benefits. For example, if the employer's location is out of London, this could be promoted as meaning that property is better value and there is beautiful countryside on the doorstep.

Name of the recruiting organisation: Robert Half International's research found that 13% of candidates would not respond to an advertisement where the recruiting organisation did not identify itself. The organisation should name itself, in order to make the most of the marketing and promotional opportunity provided by the recruitment need. However, the name should be omitted if the organisation has been experiencing some bad press (because of poor performance, for example) and its name would generally put applicants off. Similarly, if the incumbent staff member is still in the job, and does not know that they will soon be moving on, then that the advertisement should again be run blind, i.e. without disclosing the organisation's identity.

Recruiters sometimes face a choice between running an advertisement that includes the organisation's name and leaves out the salary, or that leaves out the name and includes the salary. If you really have a strong corporate brand, then you may do better to use your name and omit the salary details. However, if you do not have a particularly strong brand image, you will be better off leaving out your name but including the salary.

The essential elements above should come in the first section of the advert, ordered so as to highlight the aspect that will have most candidate impact. For example, if the role comes with a particularly high salary, say that upfront.

Advertisement layouts

A typical layout would start with the essential content above (job title, salary, location, employer name) and then include a paragraph about the organisation. This information must be tailored to reflect the target audience. For example, if recruiting for a financial role, the description could include details of turnover, profitability and share price; if recruiting for the marketing department, the paragraph could talk about new product developments and marketing initiatives.

The advertisement should then give some key information about the role itself. The aim here is to highlight any aspects that are unusual or exciting. You should not waste space on aspects that are commonly expected to be part of such a role, as the target applicants will assume these to be involved anyway.

The next section of the advertisement would typically give an indication of the type of person the organisation is trying to target. The requirements might include the kind of academic background and qualifications, as well as the characteristics of the kind of people who thrive within the organisation. Try and avoid stereotypical descriptors. For example, it is common for advertisements to say things like, 'You should be a good communicator and effective staff manager'. Unfortunately, most people find it hard to self-select themselves against such descriptions. What is a good communicator? It is better to use statements such as 'You will have had three years' experience of managing a team, with between four and 10 staff members reporting to you'.

Finally, the advertisement should end with the essential contact details. Include as wide a range of contact methods as possible: postal address, e-mail address, fax and telephone, if possible. People have their own preferences for making applications, so the advertisement should try to make life easy for everyone.

Figure 9.1 shows an advertisement we have created for the fictional vacancy at Books Plus Select that we first introduced in Chapter 7: The Recruitment Process. This advertisement is to be run in the general appointments section of a Sunday newspaper; it therefore flags up the specific role involved – Finance Director – right at the top. It also follows the golden rule of including salary and location information, and the company's name. It aims to attract applications by stressing the commercial nature of the role and the involvement in formulating strategy. The emphasis on managing change highlights the fact that this is not a role for someone who likes a static environment; given the recent merger mentioned in the first paragraph, considerable integration activity is still going on and suitable applicants will need to be able to handle that.

Advertising style

The style of any recruitment advertisement must reflect the brand image and internal culture of the recruiting organisation. This means taking care over the general presentation and the writing style of the advertisement.

• BOOKS PLUS SELECT •

Finance Director

Managing Change
c.£85,000 + car

Based in Guildford, Surrey and Rushden, Northants

Books Plus Select is a new company formed in July 2001 as a result of the successful merger between the Book Select Service division of the Nexus Publishing Group and Books Plus of W.F. Goddard. The company is the UK market leader providing a selection, distribution, selling and marketing service of books to its retail customers, most of whom are household names.

An outstanding opportunity exists for a senior finance professional to actively contribute towards the development of the business. You will find a demanding, fast moving environment where the emphasis is upon the effective management of change.

Reporting to the Managing Director and responsible for some 30 staff, you will control and direct the financial activities of the company. Advising the Managing Director on all aspects of

finance, this highly commercial role will focus on the review of management information and formulation of business strategy. Currently the company is placing considerable emphasis on the development of computer-based systems and you will be actively involved in this critical project. The job will require some travel as you will be expected to work in both the new distribution and administration centre in Northants and the sales and marketing Head Office in Surrey.

Suitable candidates will be qualified accountants possessing commercial judgement. In your current role you provide and interpret key financial data as part of the strategic decision-taking team. You also have experience of managing staff in multiple sites and have recently led or advised on the implementation of new IT systems.

Please apply directly to Brendan Wood at GKW Executive Selection, 16 Hamilton Street, St. James's, London W1. Email: Brendan.wood@gkw.com Fax: 020 7123 4567.

GKW

Figure 9.1

Advertisement size

The size of any advertisement should be appropriate to the role it promotes. Andrea Burrows says: 'Nobody wants to pay more than they need to, but if a senior role is shoe-horned into a very small ad, it creates an impression of meanness or cheapness or lack of professionalism. So the size must be appropriate. It doesn't have to be the most expensive solution, but it must be relevant to the role and the market.' In general, large advertisements will always be more eye-catching than smaller ones.

Creativity issues

There is nothing wrong with creativity in job advertising, but that creativity needs to add something to the process of attracting candidates. Using unusual graphics or images can work well, but the images need to be relevant to the people being targeted. For example, using the image of soaring eagles around a headline that says 'Highflying opportunity' is not adding much value, or even real creativity, to the advertisement. It is a visual cliché. Images of ladders, mountain climbers and chess pieces are also highly unoriginal.

Writing style

Job advertisements should be written in a way that directly addresses the reader. 'Your role will be ...' The style should generally be relatively informal, although tailored for the target audience. The advertisement should also try to convey hard facts, as opposed to making general claims. For example, many companies claim to be 'leading', but that cannot be true of all of them. If the company *is* the market leader however, as is the case for our fictional recruiter Books Select Plus in the UK, then you should clearly say so in the advert, as we have done in Figure 9.1.

Advertisements *must* address the 'what's in it for me?' question that potential applicants will be asking themselves. Organisations may think they just need to list the requirements they have of the candidates, but in fact they need to think about what requirements the candidates may have for the organisation.

Similarly, public sector organisations that have a preference for application forms sometimes state in their advertisements that CVs will not be accepted. Such blanket statements should be avoided, since they can give job-hunters the impression that the organisation is dominated by rules, regulations and generally unpleasant bureaucracy.

Humour can be considered for use in job advertising. Although the decision to move jobs is a far more serious one than the decision about which of two washing powders to buy, this does not mean that humour is always inappropriate. People looking through job advertisements want to be engaged on a human, personal level and recruiting organisations can use humorous touches to make themselves stand out. Candidates will take it as a sign that the organisation is perhaps more relaxed and less stiff and starchy than others.

Legal issues

For the vast majority of jobs, recruiters cannot specify the gender or ethnic background required in applicants. This is illegal under UK law. However, there are limited exceptions, for example, when being from a particular racial group is a genuine occupational qualification for the job, as in a dramatic performance that is striving for authenticity.

The situation is somewhat different in relation to the age of applicants. It is not currently illegal in the UK for employers to discriminate against individuals on the grounds of their age and many job advertisements do specify preferred age ranges or say they seek applicants who are 'young and energetic'. However, a law against age discrimination is set to be introduced in the UK in 2006, in line with a European Commission directive outlawing discrimination in the workplace on the basis of age, religion or sexual orientation.

Employers who want to create a positive employer brand should not wait for the legal change before abandoning ageist policies and practices in the workplace. As the proportion of older workers continues to increase in many Western countries, so ageist corporate cultures are already losing candidate appeal. The UK government's Department for Education and Employment has produced a Code of Practice, Age Diversity in Employment, which advises that, in order to ensure the best candidates apply, employers should avoid using age limits or age ranges in job advertisements. This is good advice that all recruiters should follow.

Some organisations like to make it particularly clear that they are opposed to discrimination. Public sector employers, for example, sometimes include in their advertisements a lengthy statement of the organisation's equal opportunities policy. This degree of emphasis may be laudable, but it is not really necessary. Such an approach takes up significant chunks of advertising space for little added benefit. A more reasonable approach is to include a one-line note on the equal opportunities focus in the advertisement, and then give the full policy statement in the information pack sent out to candidates who express an initial interest in the role advertised.

Newspaper variations

When choosing which of the paper-based press to use, consider what your target candidate pool will look at. If you want senior people, you probably have to use the national press. Similarly, do not just assess the merits of any particular paper or magazine by the size of its circulation. Nor is every day as good as any other for advertising in a national newspaper. For example, UK newspaper *The Guardian* is known for its Monday media supplement and accompanying media-related job advertisements. Recruiting organisations need to make sure they place their advertisement on the day most likely to reach its target audience.

Sometimes target candidates can be reached through a publication that they would not buy themselves, but that their partner would read. For example, the woman's magazine *Cosmopolitan* has started running job advertisements. Recruiters who have used this source have received applications from men as well as women. This may be because the men have casually picked up the magazine and seen the advertisements, or because their partners have seen it and encouraged their men to apply.

Advertising the same vacancy in a number of different publications may be a sensible option. However, this does not mean that exactly the same advertisement can be used in each. You may need to adjust the format or certain content to make sure you get the right message across to your target applicant pool.

For example, the advertisement's headline must reflect the nature of the publication. If the advertisement is appearing in a national newspaper, which will be browsed through by people from a wide range of disciplines, the headline should probably include the job title or function in order to catch the attention of the target group. However, if the advertisement is appearing in a trade publication, which only circulates amongst people within the target discipline, the headline should include something more eye-catching about the job. It is a waste to headline your advertisement 'Accountant wanted' if you are advertising in a weekly paper called *Accountancy Age*.

Job advertisements on the Internet

Use of the Internet for recruitment advertising is growing. According to the Chartered Institute of Personnel and Development's May 2001 Recruitment survey, more than half of organisations now use the Internet for overall recruitment. When recruiting managers, 52.6% use the Internet, not too far behind the 66.8% who use advertisements in local papers, the 61.3% who place advertisements in national papers and the 60.1% who advertise in specialist journals or the trade press.

In most cases, Internet advertising is now often used in conjunction with other, more traditional, forms of advertising. The only exceptions tend to be graduate and IT sector recruitment, where the Internet may sometimes be used in isolation.

Sector uptake

Internet advertising appears to work best where roles advertised can be described tightly. For example, the IT sector has led the way in the growth of online job advertising. It is no coincidence that computer programming skills can be easily identified (such as C++ or Java) which means that employers can convey what they are looking for in code form. Job seekers can then conduct easy searches by using those terms as key words.

In other functional areas where the job title and role description may be more nebulous, ensuring the job vacancy comes up on a candidate's search is not so easy. For example, a 'business development' role could relate to a sales or a marketing position; the related advertisement needs to be carefully written to ensure that appropriate buzzwords are included.

Alongside the IT sector, graduate recruiting over the Internet has also noticeably taken off. Today's graduates are of a generation that is fully comfortable with technology and using the Internet is a natural thing for them to do. They have used the Internet during their degree courses and so it is second nature to use to for researching job opportunities and making job applications. Many employers have stopped producing brochures for use in graduate recruitment and are now putting the entire process on the Internet.

As these graduates work their way through their careers, so it is likely that the use of the Internet for job applications and job hunting will continue to grow. Similarly, as access to the Internet continues to grow – particularly with the development of interactive television – so even more people will have the potential to search for new jobs during their leisure time. This is likely to mean a strong future for Internet recruitment advertising.

Advantages for employers

One advantage of using the Internet for recruitment advertising is that it is generally far cheaper than the traditional paper-based press. Employers can even get an Internet presence for free; publications that have their own Internet sites will automatically transfer advertisements placed in the traditional press version onto the online edition.

Another advantage of 'net-based advertising is that vacancies can be advertised extremely quickly. A Sunday paper, for example, might require copy for colour advertisements to be supplied the preceding Monday or Tuesday, with slots booked the Friday before that. In contrast, online advertisements can be posted up almost instantly. The employer simply enters the relevant data in a specially designed form, and the advertisement information is posted up straight away.

However, cost and speed is irrelevant if the online advertisements do not generate any applications. If individual employers want to compare the success of different advertising methods, they need to give different reference numbers to online and newspaper advertisements and ask candidates to quote the reference when they apply. Shana Mazin, a media consultant at AIA, says: 'We advised one client to set up a different e-mail address for online applicants to use, just so they could monitor its use.'

Such information can also be used to assess the quality of applications received. The comparative ease of making online applications means that employers may receive more applications from less focused applicants. However, if this is a problem, some means of weeding out timewasters can be built into the process. For example, simply asking candidates to answer a couple of specific questions about themselves may be enough to put some off. Alternatively, candidates can be asked to complete an online application form, rather than just attaching a CV. The extra effort required should cut down on applications from people who are applying a blanket, 'apply for everything' approach to their job search.

Internet job advertisements can also give employers information on the success, or otherwise, of their advertisements. For example, it is possible to monitor how many people looked at a particular advertisement online – something which is impossible for newspaper advertisements – and then see what percentage clicked again to get further information and then how many followed through with an application. This level of measurability is not achievable with traditional press advertising.

Advantages for candidates

Online job advertisements can be attractive for job-hunters for several reasons. As explained above, if job roles can be clearly defined, then job-hunters can conduct highly targeted searches to try and match their needs with vacancies. Many specialist job sites also offer the facility for job seekers to register their interest so that if suitable vacancies come in, they can receive an e-mail to tell them. This means they do not have to be quite as proactive in seeking out new vacancies. If they want to research a company, the job advertisement will often direct them to the corporate website, or to backup information provided by the website host.

Once a candidate has decided to apply, e-mailing a CV is easier than having to address an envelope, find a stamp and go to the post box. Alternatively, completing an application on screen and e-mailing it in is also relatively straightforward; some information can probably be cut and pasted from the candidate's CV to reduce typing time.

Internet advertising issues

Despite the advantages of using the Internet for job advertising, this does not mean that the Internet is always the right approach for advertising, or that it can be used in isolation. Shana Mazin of AIA says: 'Internet-based advertising has got to be part of an integrated campaign, alongside other media such as the press or events such as exhibitions and open days. If companies jump in and start placing Internet ads without thinking it through properly, they can end up doing more harm than good; they may well not get the results they were promised.'

Candidates' expectations of the recruitment process may be different when they respond to an Internet advertisement. For example, since the Internet is associated with speed of access to information, candidates using it to apply for jobs probably expect to receive a faster response from the recruiter than they would if using traditional methods. Furthermore, candidates are far more likely to expect to be able to apply online, rather than having to make a postal application. Therefore, employers using the Internet to advertise vacancies need to bear this in mind in setting up an appropriate recruitment process. Shana Mazin says: 'I know of one company which was approached directly by a website and decided just to put the same advert on the web that they would have used in the press. In that ad they told interested job seekers to phone for an application form. But people using the Internet to look for jobs don't want to phone for a form, they want to just click and get it. This company didn't give people that option and the advert bombed. They had hardly any responses.'

This does not mean that applications should be requested by e-mail only. Many job-hunters search for jobs online but then apply off line. This may be because they want time to think about their application or because they are searching during their lunch hour from their current employer's offices. Sending an e-mail application from work may not be possible. Therefore some people may still prefer to download a form and send it in by post. The key point for employers is that they need to give people the widest range of options.

Organisations also need to think about how they handle responses. For example, candidates do not like it when they hear nothing at all in response to their application, but receiving too fast a rejection may also leave them with a bad feeling about that organisation. Shana Mazin says: 'When using the Internet you can get people to complete online questionnaires, which can help sift out unsuitable applicants. But this means that people can receive virtually automatic rejections almost before they have applied. What kind of image does that give them of the company? It doesn't make the applicants feel good.'

Writing Internet advertisements

All job advertisements need to be punchy, but advertisements designed for the Internet need to be even more so. Robert Peasnell of McCann-Erickson says: 'We generally find that online ads may be around 25% shorter than normal press advertisements. That's because browsers don't want to have to scroll down, so the text needs to fit on the screen. That means you need to write short, pithy ads that grab the attention. They may then, of course, lead on to other sites that include a lot more information on the job and the organisation.'

Given that candidates will try searching to identify appropriate vacancies, key words must be included. The text should include all the relevant skills sets. Salary and location information should always be included if possible, as candidates often use these for their search criteria.

The corporate website

Employers who want to use the Internet to attract candidates for vacant positions can do so by advertising jobs on their own corporate website – generally on a recruitment micro site that sits behind the main site – or by using the facilities of a specialist recruitment jobsite.

Employers who develop their own recruitment micro sites recognise that many job seekers have in mind the specific organisation that they would like to work for. Such job seekers who have Internet access will often want to look at their target organisation's website. Generation X members are attracted by strong brands, for example, and so are likely to visit an organisation's website simply to look for job vacancies. By making sure such browsers find vacancies displayed on the corporate website, the employer can tap straight into this willing talent pool.

Using a recruitment micro site allows key vacancy and selection information to be contained in a dedicated area, but with links to the main site so that the job seekers can research the organisation, its performance and culture in depth. Some employers are specifically targeting graduates in this way, establishing a dedicated section catering to their needs, with its own precise web address.

Employers can still have their own recruitment micro sites and also use third party recruitment websites to drive traffic to them. They can put their advertised vacancies and a couple of paragraphs about the organisation on the third party site and then include a link through to their own site, where candidates can find a lot more information on the culture of the organisation and the department.

Job sites work in different ways, however. Some like to keep job seekers on their own website. In such cases, advertisers are encouraged to put more of their recruitment information on the job site, instead of providing a link to their own corporate website. Employers will have to bear this issue in mind when deciding which job sites to use.

Choosing an Internet job site

There are many Internet recruitment sites around at the moment. They differ in a number of ways. First, there are the generalist, or horizontal, sites (such as monster.com, stepstone. com or gojobsite.co.uk) and the specialist, or vertical, sites (such as jobsfinancial.com or retailcareer.com).

Generalists cover a broad range of industry sectors and jobs. The advantage is that they often have a high profile, generated by extensive advertising campaigns. However, their potential downside is that they are trying to be all things to all people; they may generate high levels of traffic, attracting job seekers from a wide range of disciplines, but there is a risk that the needs of many will be unfulfilled. If people do not find what they want as an initial visitor they may not return again.

The specialist sector sites have the advantage of being focused on a specific group of job hunters, and therefore may have a better chance of providing something they are looking for. Some sites (such as accountingweb.co.uk) combine advertising vacancies with extensive editorial comment on news and events in the sector, giving web surfers an added incentive to visit the site.

Robert Peasnell says: 'I expect there to be a rationalisation in the marketplace over the next couple of years, with the market coming down to two or three big destination recruitment sites, plus a lot of smaller specialist sites. The sites that are proving most successful for us at the moment are not so much the big corporate sites, but the more narrowly targeted sites that are almost like the trade press online; they are specific sites servicing a discrete audience and are sites that people in the sector have a reason to visit editorially, to read news and comment. While they are there they may do a job search as well, so you get more passive job-hunters who may then make an application if they see something that interests them.'

There is also a difference between job sites in the way that they operate, as we said above. Shana Mazin says: 'Sites work in different ways. Some want to keep the job searcher on their site for as long as possible. Others will be quite happy to let the employer have a link to their own website. Employers have to look at their own recruitment campaign and decide what is best for them.'

The models used by recruitment advertising websites also vary. For example, many charge a fee per number of advertisements for a specified period, with the average rate per job advertisement falling the more advertisements are posted. Extra charges may be made for specified extra services, such as adding corporate profiles or corporate branding opportunities on the site.

Top Jobs on the Net (www.topjobs.co.uk) is a general recruitment advertising site, but has an unusual model in that it requires employers to subscribe for a year's service. Fees range from around £6000 for a one-page slot appropriate to a small business, to £120,000 for 60 slots. Although relatively expensive in Internet advertising terms, the fees still compare well with national newspaper advertising charges.

Kay Wesley, Vice President of Corporate Operations and Strategy, Top Jobs on the Net, says: 'Top Jobs' approach is to give the employer a platform on which they can tell the candidate about the company and the job. We work with each client to try and make each campaign work. For a year's subscription the employer gets a number of slots, and can put a job

117

advertisement into each one. They get templates that use the company branding. Once a client subscribes the official lead-time to set them up is six days, but it never takes that long. Our record was one hour and 40 minutes.' Corporate information is also all contained on the Top Jobs site. Text and graphic pages are designed in the client company's style to promote its employer brand. The Top Jobs front page can also run new stories about the client, designed to attract applicants' attention.

Top Jobs' subscribers can place advertisements as and when they choose. Kay Wesley says: 'HR people find they can take control of the process – they can tinker with the ad to get the response they want; if they are getting too many applications they can adjust the advert to highlight certain qualities that are mandatory. They can change the ad from day to day and exploit the interactive element.' Top Jobs was launched in the UK in April 1996. In August 2001, the IT sector claimed the largest number of applications on the site (7352), resulting from 192,000 page views of those jobs. In other words, the IT advertisements were viewed on average 26 times per application. There was also strong activity in the following sectors: sales and business development (6201 applications), engineering (3816), banking and finance (2926), graduate recruitment (2852) and consultancy (2834).

As a recruiting employer, once you have decided on the type of site you want to use, you need to assess its efficiency and effectiveness. Shana Mazin says: 'Look at how many jobs they have on the site and make sure the site is updated. Traffic figures are important, but are not the be all and end all. Sites that generate the most traffic don't necessarily have the highest rate of applications. What counts is that when people get onto the site they find what they want, and so they are more likely to apply.'

Advertising errors

Most organisations have experience of highly successful advertising campaigns, as well as those that flop. Job advertising can go wrong, particularly if inadequate time is allowed for planning the advertising strategy and drafting advertisements that convey the right attraction signals to appropriate candidates.

Andrea Burrows of AIA says that organisations can often be guilty of giving advertising agencies inadequate time to prepare for the advertising they need; an individual may resign, but the advertising agency is not told until three weeks later. She says: 'Taking the brief, making sure the corporate ID is right, developing the message and the employer brand promise or personality that comes through – that all takes time. More time spent planning, understanding the proposition and choosing the appropriate media, would be time well spent.'

Apart from inadequate planning, other common errors include:

- omitting the salary without good reason;
- failing to include indicators that signal who the advertisement is designed for;
- using inappropriate or hackneyed creativity that adds nothing to the message;
- giving vague descriptions of the kind of person the organisation is looking for;
- giving applicants inadequate or inappropriate options for making their applications (for example, by post only).

By following the advice given earlier in this chapter, you should be able to avoid making these kinds of mistakes.

Handling advertisement responses

Employers need to try and make the advertising and applicant response process as personal as possible. Of course, this is difficult if an advertisement triggers 250 applications; many HR departments simply do not have the manpower to send out hundreds of rejection letters.

Sometimes organisations include a line in the advertisement to the effect that 'We regret that only successful candidates will be contacted'. This may be realistic, but organisations should be aware that it could put some applicants off. This could not only damage the recruitment campaign, but also have a bad impact on the employer and corporate brand; it could even potentially lose the organisation the goodwill of candidates who also happen to be customers. That said, not giving such a message and then simply ignoring unsuitable applications will not create a very good impression either.

It is striking how few recruiters actually do respond to candidate applications. Robert Half International conducted research to see whether there was any difference in the way employers treated speculative applications from people of different genders or races. Although there was no noticeable difference, there was another striking finding: only around a third of companies even acknowledged receiving the applications. These were largely companies with household names who almost certainly attract applications precisely because people use and like their goods and services. These companies may have mission statements that highlight their customer focus, but when it comes to dealing with customers who want to become employees, that theoretical customer focus disappears.

Advertising is an important part of the process of perception and reputation management. If the advertisement is professional, so must letters inviting applicants to interview be written professionally. This is an essential part of the employer branding process. One of these applicants will, if all goes well, join the organisation at the end of the recruitment campaign. Their perceptions will start being formed from the moment their eye first catches the headline of the advertisement. If they are positively attracted at that moment, you want them to still be feeling positive when they turn up for work on day one.

We consider the process of reviewing applications in the next chapter.

Chapter 10

CVs and Application Forms

I n the private sector, most recruiters simply ask for applicants to send in their CVs in order to be considered for an interview, whereas most public sector and voluntary organisations require them to fill in application forms.

There are pros and cons attached to both approaches, so which is best for you?

Application forms or CVs?

Some recruiters, notably those in public sector organisations, may decide that CVs are not the best sources of information when choosing candidates for interview. They may prefer to require applicants to complete standardised application forms.

Application forms can have the following advantages:

- They help to create a 'level playing field' when identifying suitable candidates for interview.
- Candidates can be required to answer specific questions designed to highlight relevant competencies.
- Applicants who complete the form have already demonstrated a degree of motivation and enthusiasm for the job.

The 'level playing field' aspect is one major reason why application forms are favoured in the public sector where, as we pointed out in Chapter 7: The Recruitment Process, considerable attention is given to equal opportunity issues. The fact that all applicants have to provide information on specified issues should make it easier for recruiters to pick out those with the most relevant experience. This can provide extra reassurance that the recruitment process is being managed in an objective and fair manner that minimises the risk of discrimination.

However, there are counterbalancing disadvantages to using application forms:

- Extra effort is required to design the form.
- Failing to tailor the form for each vacancy can result in meaningless information being required.
- Some candidates may be put off by the extra effort required to complete an application form, as opposed to simply sending in a CV.

The fact that some candidates may be put off could also be an advantage to the employer if a huge response to a job advertisement is anticipated. Requiring application forms to be completed can act as a useful self-screening tool, saving the recruiter time in reading through applications.

Some recruiters might also say that if a candidate is put off by having to complete a form, then that candidate does not deserve the job. But it may be that the candidates who are most likely to be put off are the best ones, who have most career choices. Even worse, what if you suspect there is only a small pool of applicants potentially suitable for the position? One UK government department found that 70% of all forms requested were not returned. With this kind of fall-out rate you could be seriously limiting your choices, particularly if you are fishing among a small number of qualified candidates. The most qualified person for the job could be interested in your opportunity, but simply too busy to be able to spend time doing the form justice.

In this case, you might want to avoid using an application form and request CVs in order to maximise the initial application tally. Applications can always be introduced as a second stage screening mechanism if numerous applicants express initial interest in the vacancy. Alternatively, give applicants a choice between answering the questions in the form, or sending in their CV and extra supporting information.

Hamish Davidson, Partner and Head of the UK Executive Search and Selection Division at PricewaterhouseCoopers, suggests that recruiting organisations, including public sector and voluntary organisations, should question whether they really need to use an application form at all, even if this has been the established norm. He says: 'We advise clients to drop application forms. Instead we would ask candidates to submit a CV and supporting documents.' Those documents must address the appointment criteria given in the information pack, making clear the candidate's suitability in the required competency areas. If a client still insists on using an application form, then Davidson suggests that candidates be given a choice between completing it or submitting their CV and supporting documentation that addresses the job criteria.

Monitoring forms

Whether or not an application form is used, candidates should be asked to complete a separate monitoring form. This gathers information on facts such as the ethnic background, disability and age of candidates and is designed to help organisations assess their equal opportunities performance.

Monitoring forms should be separated from application forms on receipt, and play no part in the selection process. They are simply used for information purposes. Collecting such data has until recently been a matter of best practice only. However, under the UK's Race Relations (Amendment) Act 2000, over 300 public authorities and bodies now have a general duty to work towards the elimination of racial discrimination. Where private sector organisations have taken over some of these public sector bodies' functions, then the private sector employers too should take up that general duty.

In practice this means that public sector bodies, and affected private sector organisations, must monitor the ethnic composition of their workforce to ensure that it reflects the ethnic composition of the local community. Making use of monitoring forms to establish the ethnic composition of job applicants is a vital stage of this process. Data on applicants can be compared to data on successful recruits. This can help to highlight whether the recruitment process is discriminatory in any way, or whether enough is being done to attract applications from members of minority ethnic groups.

Designing application forms

If you decide to use application forms, it is important to design them well.

Gary Hoyte, an HR Consultant and formerly HR Director of Scope, says: 'Application forms bring major benefits for recruiters, but they have to be designed properly. If the form is well-designed and seems relevant to the position, it will enhance the image of the organisation. On the other hand, if it is wordy and just seems to be a standard form that's used for all vacancies, it won't make a good impression.'

When designing the application form, be careful to:

- avoid making it too long;
- plan your question order and spacing carefully;
- focus on areas where written information provides real evidence;
- make it clear what you are looking for;
- enable candidates to access and complete them electronically.

Problems of length
As we have explained, the requirement to complete and application form can easily deter candidates. Long forms are particularly off-putting. Keep the form focused on deriving the information you really need from candidates.

Question order
Ask questions in an order that will appear logical to candidates and make sure you allow sufficient space for them to answer.

Focus on areas where written information provides real evidence
The evidence requested in the form should be appropriate to the format and written media in general, such as providing details of past work experience and achievements. PricewaterhouseCoopers' policy is to create a two-part candidate specification. Hamish Davidson explains: 'Part I contains the essential information that you can judge in written form, that can be considered objectively; and Part II relates to all the things you can't possibly judge in writing, but can only assess in person at an interview, such as the ability to think on your feet, or a commitment to the ethos of the public sector.'

Part I should ideally relate to no more than 10 required criteria for the candidate to address. Part II should set out what else the recruiter is looking for, and that these competencies will be looked for at any subsequent interview.

Make it clear what you are looking for
When you send out the application forms explain how they will be used and why candidates should spend time thinking about the information they supply.

'Employers can be very secretive about what they are looking for,' says Chris Tanner, Independent Business Consultant and former Director of Training at Deloitte and Touche. 'You should communicate exactly what you are looking for and then challenge candidates to show they have it. You shouldn't try and be subversive or mysterious about what you want.'

Electronic access and completion
Paper-based forms are no longer appropriate in a world where many applicants will have access to neither old-fashioned typewriters nor scanners: without either, candidates have to handwrite their answers, an anachronistic requirement in an age when the majority of written communication is now in typed form.

Gary Hoyte advises: 'Application forms need to be accessible online, not just so that applicants can print them off and complete them manually, but so that they can complete them electronically. This can significantly reduce the hassle for applicants. They may even be able to cut and paste some information straight from their CVs onto the form.'

Selecting candidates from CVs and application forms

The candidate's CV or application will probably be the first source of information that the recruiting organisation has about job candidates. Knowing what to look for can improve the efficiency with which recruiters select those for interview, and the questions they then ask them.

Imagine you have been charged with coming up with a short-list for a first round interview. It is Monday morning, you have a coffee in your hand and a pile of CVs (or completed application forms) on your desk. How do you go about sifting through them?

The following tips may help:

- refer to the job description and candidate profile;
- look for desired competencies and evidence of relevant experience and achievements;
- place most emphasis on recent experience;
- review with a pen in hand;
- scan for evidence, do not read every word;
- be on the look out for vague words or qualifying statements;
- watch out for unexplained gaps in work experience or illogical job moves;

Refer to the job description and candidate profile
CVs and application forms cannot be read in isolation. They are only useful sources of information when reviewed in the light of the particular job description and candidate profile drawn up for this vacancy. It is irrelevant how many prizes someone has won for public speaking, if this job requires them to be in a back office role with little interpersonal contact.

Look for desired competencies and evidence of relevant experience and achievements
Throughout the process of reviewing the CVs and forms, maintain a detective's mind-set. You are looking for evidence of suitability for the job. The information given in the CV or form should make it clear why the candidate is suitable for the job, by indicating competencies appropriate to the role. Those competencies should be clearly evidenced by the information given on past roles and achievements. Concentrate on the 'must have' items first. 'Nice to have' competencies can be taken into account if you find you have a plentiful choice of suitable applicants.

Some recruiters, particularly those in the public sector using application forms, formalise the matching of applicants' competencies to the job criteria by using a matrix format: candidates' names can be listed down one side, and each element of the job specification along the other. Well-designed application forms should make the process of identifying suitable candidates in this way more straightforward. Applicants with the most ticks against their names are then invited for interview. This may seem highly mechanistic, but it is designed to minimise subjective influences in the decision process and to concentrate selectors' minds on looking for real evidence of suitability for the job. It also ensures that irrelevant factors (such as age, gender, race or disability) are not allowed to cloud the decision-making process.

Place most emphasis on recent experience
The applicant's current role is the one that deserves most attention. Look for similarities that suggest the experience gained will be appropriate for the vacancy to be filled. Consider whether applying for this vacant position makes sense in terms of the candidate's career plan. If not, look for an explanation as to why the applicant believes he or she can do this job and deserves to be appointed.

Review with a pen in hand
Do not sit passively reading. Use a pen to mark up the CVs and application forms as you go through them. You could, for example, simply tick aspects of work experience that suggest this applicant fits the candidate profile. If something seems unclear, mark it with a question mark. Ring any information that might need clarifying or make notes in the margin on issues to be followed up at a subsequent interview.

Scan for evidence; do not read every word
Recruitment consultants who spend many hours reviewing CVs have learnt not to spend too much time agonising over each one.

Suzzane Wood, Partner and Head of the Financial Management Practice at Executive Search Consultants Odgers Ray and Berndtson, says: 'I don't want to read 100 CVs word for word. I just look for whether they are screaming that they are right for the job. I want to see what they are currently doing, how much they are earning, where they live and what their track record is. But their current role is by far the most important and relevant.'

A general scan of the CV may also give some clues as to the personality of the applicant and the aspects of work achievements that are most important. Simon Howard, *Sunday Times*

Job File Columnist and an expert on recruitment and employment matters, says: 'The CV will give you an impression of what the candidate sees as important. For example, do the key achievements tend to focus on cost savings? Or are they more closely related to people issues, team building and staff development? You can also get a sense of whether the candidate is preoccupied with detail or with big picture issues, as well as hard evidence of writing ability.'

Be on the look out for vague words and qualifying statements
The candidates' objective will be to present themselves in the most favourable light. This inevitably means that some will try to dress up minor achievements or peripheral involvement in projects to make them look far more impressive than they actually were.

Suggested vague words and phrases to look out for include:

- 'assisted with', as in 'I assisted with the development of a major marketing initiative.' Does this mean that the applicant came up with some of the creative ideas, or merely photocopied background research material for the key decision-makers?
- 'involved in', as in 'I was involved in the implementation of a firm-wide knowledge base.' Did the applicant get involved in the project management, or simply source a list of potential IT consultants?
- 'knowledge of', as in 'I developed knowledge of international tax issues.' From reading a tax journal? Or did the applicant actually work on tax computations for the company's international operations?
- 'exposure to', as in 'I had exposure to strategic HR planning'. Was the candidate involved in the planning, or merely sat next to the person who did it?

Vague language may not necessarily rule someone out of the interview pile, but such phrases should be highlighted for probing if they are passed through to the next stage.

Watch out for unexplained gaps in work experience or illogical job moves
In the same way that recruiters should be on the look out for vague words and phrases, gaps in work experience should also

be noted for follow-up at interview. It may be that the applicant was made redundant for reasons beyond their control, or was off sick. Perhaps they had decided on a career change and just took time to find the right job. Whatever the reason, recruiters should find out to avoid any nasty surprises emerging down the line.

Common reviewing mistakes

Try to avoid the following common mistakes:

- Being distracted by what appears to be impressive experience, but experience that is not relevant to the vacancy in question.
- Comparing CV with CV, rather than against the job description.
- Being overly influenced by presentation rather than substance.
- Ruling someone out purely on grounds of age.
- Making assumptions about candidates purely based on age, sex or race.

These mistakes all basically result from a single error in approach: failing to focus on looking for evidence of competencies that match the candidate profile. If you can keep the candidate profile to the forefront of your mind as you review, the chances are that the outcome will be a list of applicants with appropriate skills, expertise and competencies who are worthy of an invitation to an interview.

In Figure 10.1, we give an example of a CV sent in by a fictional Arthur Smith in response to a fictional advertised vacancy at imaginary company Books Plus Select, shown in Figure 9.1.

A quick scan of Arthur's CV suggests he could be worth interviewing. He currently holds a commercial role, and a commercial focus is important to Books Plus Select. At the interview stage, it would be worth investigating how much strategic input he has in his current company. Arthur also has been involved with the successful development of a new computer system for his current employer. However, he does not actually say how closely he was involved or what he actually did in this process, and so this would be an issue to follow up at interview.

ARTHUR BERNARD SMITH

Personal	Date of Birth – 4.4.62 Married
Education	1973–1978 Salesian College, Chertsey 7 'O' Level G.C.E. Passes
	1978–1980 Dauntsey's School, Wiltshire 2 'O' Level G.C.E. Passes 2 'A' Level G.C.E. Passes
	1980–1984 West London University B.A. (2 : 2) – Business Studies
Professional qualifications	Chartered Accountant

Position history

Feb 1995–Present

International Global Pictures, London W6
Marketing, sales and distribution of approximately 40% of all American films, producing a turnover of $400 million. The company employs some 1500 people located in the major capitals of the world.

Director, Commercial Accounting
Responsible for four departments, namely Management Reporting, Licensor Reporting, Release Cost Control and Sales Statistics.

All departments are involved in the preparation, review and analysis of all management information for the group. This includes the annual budget, monthly management reporting, appraisals of individual film performances and the analysis of detailed sales and marketing information.

Information is reviewed with operational vice presidents where improvements to operational efficiency can be planned and executed.

The successful development of new computer systems.

Active member of the Senior Management Team, giving commercial support and direction where necessary. The development and training of all staff members. The position is responsible for 22 members of staff.

Achievements
The implementation of a new computer system on licensor and release cost reporting, reducing time needed to report information and facilitating greater use of this information in forecasting.

The successful negotiation of an international advertising agency relationship to improve the servicing of our needs and to produce major cost savings to IGP in reduced fees and cheaper purchases of media.

Release Costs Controller
To ensure all costs are strictly controlled by the review of sales and marketing budgets and subsequent analysis of expenditure. The review and selection of advertising agencies and major suppliers

Figure 10.1

130

worldwide to ensure the company obtained the desired services at the lowest cost.

To provide commercial support to the Sales and Marketing Departments and to comment on levels of expenditure against projection income estimates. This includes, as an example, the evaluation of new markets and the assessment of new advertising and promotional activities.

Achievements
Setting up of a new department to provide an improved level of control over these costs.

A 'value for money' approach with suppliers resulting in cost savings in the region of $250,000 per annum.

Oct 1991–Jan 1995 **CBA Records Division, London WC1**
The division had a turnover of approximately £50 million and employed some 275 people.

June 1992–Jan 1995 **Commercial Manager**
During this period achieved the successful negotiation of a new manufacturing agreement whereby singles were supplied to CBA at significantly reduced prices – estimated savings of £500,000 over two years.

Also re-negotiated distribution and selling arrangement with UK's major TV merchandising company, ensuring highest ever yearly profits from this source contributing in excess of £1 million profit.

Sept 1992–June 1993 **Manager, Finance Planning and Analysis**
Monthly forecasts of profits cash and balance sheets. Preparation of annual budgets. Continuous review of all profit centres. Daily liaison with all operating departments.

During this period totally redesigned the management reporting, dividing the company into profit centres.

Oct 1991–Sept 1992 **Chief Accountant**
Responsibility for day to day accounting aspects of the company. Review and update of systems and control procedures. During this period introduced revised policies for evaluating provisions on inventories and recording costs and also a meaningful variance analysis on operating costs.

Feb 1990–Oct 1991 **TIP LTD, London**
Assistant to Group Chief Accountant
Preparation of monthly board profits after analysis of subsidiary reporting packages. Annual Consolidation of 26 overseas companies.

During this employment introduced tighter working capital reporting aiding a £6 million improvement to the group's cash flow.

Sept 1984–Feb 1990 **Coopers and Lomax, London**
Three year training contract and additional experience as audit supervisor.

Other activities Tennis, swimming, snooker, walking. Member of the National Geographical Society.

Potential problems

Even having followed the key reviewing tips, the CV reviewer may still be faced with one of two problems: too many potential interview candidates, or not enough of them. Most professional recruitment consultants will aim to invite around 12 people to first round interviews after an initial review of their CVs or application forms. What happens if you are too far off this mark?

Too many interview candidates

If you end up with too long a list of names, in a sense this is good news, as it suggests that there is a plentiful supply of people who could potentially suit the role. However, do you really want to interview 15 or 20 people?

It's probably worth spending a little more time now quickly going through those 20 CVs again and whittling them down by half. There are probably some obvious favourites and some people who, on second thoughts, do not appear quite as impressive as they did at first sight. Do some candidates have more of the 'nice to have' competencies and qualities than others?

If the process still seems impossible, and everyone remaining on the list appears equally suitable, focus on other data such as current address. Someone living locally is probably a better bet than someone currently based at the other end of the country. It is also worth double-checking that you have not included people who are overqualified, as their salary expectations may ultimately prove too high. If the candidate has included some information on hobbies and pastimes, do they shed any light on suitability? If someone clearly enjoys team sports, does this suggest they will fit in well with the department's strong team culture? At the last resort, look for any indications of enthusiasm; passion for the job is an indicator of potential high performance.

If you really cannot whittle the CV pile down to a suitable number, consider a halfway house option – contacting some of the question mark candidates by phone. A 10-minute, relatively informal, chat to probe any areas of doubt should help identify those really worth meeting in person and those not quite suitable enough.

Too few candidates

But what if the review of CVs has left you with just a handful of preferred interview candidates? Is it too risky to limit your options in this way?

It is worth double-checking that you have not been unnecessarily harsh in your review of the CVs or allowed personal preferences or bias to rule out suitable people. However, if you have focused on identifying suitable competences then the chances are you have achieved a sensible result. In recruitment, it is quality rather than quantity that counts. Even if only one person meets your needs, as long as you can persuade that person that you are the employer for them, that is all that counts.

That said, you do not want to make yourself hostage to fortune. Try to interview at least a handful of people, even if there is one obvious candidate that you know you really want. We now move on to consider the interview process in detail. Although interviews form the key element of most selection processes, many recruiters fail to get the best results from them. We aim to put that right.

Chapter 11

Interviewing: Technique Tips

There are three things in life that people generally refuse to admit they are bad at: driving, making love and finally, conducting an interview. We cannot promise to help with the first two, but hope this chapter will give some useful advice on how to interview.

The problem with interviews

Interviews are the most commonly used selection technique in the recruitment process, but they are rarely performed as effectively as they could be. Interviewers frequently fail to find out the real information they need for effective selection. This is most often the case because interviewers:

- are under-prepared;
- talk too much;
- make premature decisions based on first, instinctive reactions;
- do not take notes;
- have designed no structure behind their questions;
- should not be interviewing in the first place.

Many of these mistakes arise because interviewers are failing to apply the key pointers outlined later in this chapter. However, the final problem – choosing the wrong person to be the interviewer – is in a different class. This is an issue that the HR team must address in their up-front planning for the selection process. Someone will be inappropriate as an interviewer if they cannot convey the desired employer brand effectively. We highlighted the importance of this in Chapter 7: The Recruitment Process, under the section on 'Selecting the right selectors'.

However, interviewers will also be the wrong people for the job if they have never been trained in interviewing techniques.

Most people assume that they know how to interview people. After all, it is about talking, is it not?

The truth is that interviewing is a skill. One of the main problems with the interview as a selection tool is that many line managers who find themselves interviewing job candidates have never had any training in this most critical activity. Informal samples of seminar groups generally indicate that perhaps one in four managers has ever benefited from any training on how to conduct an effective interview.

Moreover, training in interview techniques tends to be voluntary. Those who actually sign up for the training are generally those who are already reasonably good at it, appreciate the complexities involved and who are motivated to improve their skill. Those who are poor interviewers or who assume they know what they are doing are far less likely to ask for the training. HR departments should consider making interview training a compulsory course for managers of a certain level who are likely to be spending time in their careers selecting others to work for the organisation. At the least, they could learn some useful communication skills with even wider applicability than in the formal selection interview.

However, if you have not had any interview training and you have got to assess a few candidates tomorrow, our 10-point plan for interview effectiveness should go some way to improving the likely outcome.

The 10-point plan for interview effectiveness

There are three key outcomes that you want to achieve by the end of the interview. First, you need to have found evidence that justifies the candidate's suitability for the job. The candidate's CV will have made a series of claims that were sufficiently impressive to win them an interview; your job in the interview is to find confirmatory evidence that backs up those claims.

Secondly, at the end of every interview you want candidates to be left with a positive impression. You want each candidate to feel they want to work for your organisation, whether or not you think them suitable.

Thirdly, you want to make sure the candidate has realistic expectations about the organisation and the role. You do not want to give someone such an inflated, rosy picture that when they join they feel they have been, in a sense, sold a dud.

You stand the best chance of achieving these two aims if you follow these 10 key steps:

1. do your preparation;
2. stick to your interview agenda;
3. choose an appropriate environment;
4. relax the interviewee;
5. ask effective questions;
6. encourage the candidate to talk;
7. be a conscious listener;
8. note down key information;
9. play the attraction game;
10. close the meeting professionally.

1. *Do your preparation*

Sometimes the simplest things are the hardest to do. Ask anyone what they should do before conducting an interview, and the answer will be a textbook reply: review the CV and identify areas for questioning.

What really happens?
It is 9.50 a.m. and your receptionist has just rung to say the 10-o' clock-interview candidate has arrived. You are in the midst of dictating a budget memo, which you want typed up in advance of a team meeting later in the day. You tell the receptionist to offer the interviewee a tea or coffee and say you will be down to collect them shortly. Fifteen minutes later you finally finish with the memo and dig out the candidate's CV from the pile of paper on your desk. It is vaguely familiar, because luckily you did look at it a week ago when agreeing the interview short-list. You flick your eyes over it again for 10 seconds, double check the chap's name and race off to reception. Having collected your candidate, you decide to get the candidate talking to give yourself time to think up some specific questions.

'Tell me about yourself', you say. 'Why are you interested in this job?'

And so it is that responsibility for the success of the interview and control over its direction has been shifted right over to the candidate.

Such behaviour may be understandable, but it is not the way to maximise the effectiveness of the interview. The message is constantly hammered home to interview candidates that they must prepare, prepare, prepare. In our job-hunting guide, *Kickstart Your Career*, we repeatedly emphasise to applicants that they must research their prospective employer, think about the questions they could be asked and practice sample answers.[1] This is a lot of effort. The same degree of attention to the recruitment process must be shown by the recruiting organisation, and that particularly means the interviewer.

Enough lecturing. What should this preparation involve?

Realistically, 10 minutes is probably all the time a busy manager can spare to look over the CV or application form and structure the most appropriate interview questions. But a lot of planning can be achieved in 10 minutes. To make sure that this time does not get swallowed up by an urgent task requiring your attention immediately before the interview, it is sensible to make interview planning your first activity of the day. Get your coffee or tea and, before doing anything else, do your interview preparation. Jot down your agenda, as described in step 2, and plan your questions.

In Chapter 10: CVs and Application Forms, we looked at the types of things to look out for when selecting appropriate interview candidates. We also suggested highlighting areas for follow-up at interview. As a recap, when preparing interview questions, remember to

- focus on areas of most relevance to the vacant role;
- pay more attention to the candidate's recent experience;
- design your key questions with an emphasis on desired competencies (but remember you will need to develop follow-up questions on the hoof during the interview, depending what the candidate says);

- make a note to look behind vague words and phrases – aim to find out what the candidate actually did that added value to their employing organisation;
- investigate any gaps in employment or illogical career moves.

Planning in this way means that your interview will have some structure. This is important when you are interviewing several candidates, since it increases the chance that you can compare like with like. If you have done no planning, have no structure and do not know what aspects of the candidates' experience needs to be investigated, how can you choose who is most suitable for the job?

2. Stick to your interview agenda

An interview should follow a logical progression. Too often, as a result of inadequate planning, interviewers allow them to take a meandering, unstructured course where information is gathered in a haphazard manner.

Our recommended interview structure would be as follows:

- greet the candidate;
- outline the interview agenda;
- move on to the main questioning stage;
- describe the organisation and the vacant position in a way that sells the opportunity;
- answer the candidate's questions;
- close the interview (as described in step 10).

Establishing such a structure enables the interviewer to remain in control of the interview and maximises the potential for obtaining the desired information about the candidate.

When outlining the interview agenda, the interviewer should indicate that the primary aim is to find out more about the candidate and their potential suitability, particularly their past experience, achievements and behaviours. This introductory stage should not turn into a description of the organisation, the department and the role to be filled, which should be left until the interviewer's key questions have been asked. Giving such detail up-front simply means that the astute candidate can shape their answers to match what the interviewer has just told them, rather than giving a more true impression of themselves.

As the interview progresses, keep your objectives in mind. Keep an eye on the clock so that you avoid running out of time. You do not want to find that you have only covered half your key issues. If you want a candidate to speed up their answers or give more detail, ask them politely to do so. You are the one who should be in control of the interview.

In terms of how long to spend on an interview, candidates will generally expect an hour-long session. If you close the interview after just half an hour they may assume they have not done well, or think the organisation is being unprofessional by rushing the interview process. A sensible approach is to state up-front that you expect the interview to last for around 45 minutes. If you establish quickly that this candidate is clearly unsuitable, you can still end the interview after 35–40 minutes, and the candidate will not notice. However, if the candidate is interesting and the interview overruns to an hour, they will probably leave punching the air because they know the session has gone well.

3. *Choose an appropriate environment*

The interview environment is extremely important. Ushering a candidate into a poky meeting room littered with old coffee cups and ash trays will make an extremely poor impression. Interviewing is about attracting as well as assessing, and so the environment must be selected with care.

With the spread of open plan offices many managers no longer have their own private space. But even if the interviewer does have their own private room, it is still better to select more neutral territory; candidates may feel at a disadvantage, and therefore more stressed, if they feel they are being interviewed in the midst of your power base.

Experienced recruiter Dr Gareth Jones, formerly Director of HR and Internal Communications at the BBC, certainly advocates using a setting where the power relationship between the interviewer and interviewee disappears, although he likes to apply his own twist to this. He says: 'Never interview in your own office. However, meeting rooms are usually pretty awful, so I try and put people in a slightly unusual setting if I can, to try and get them slightly off guard. A lot of people expect to be stressed in interviews, but they do not expect to be stressed in the pub, or over a coffee. I used to meet people in a café near the BBC or in a pub. We were once recruiting someone from the film industry and I had arranged to meet her for a drink in a pub near Broadcasting House. After I had grilled her for an hour and a half – a serious intellectual grilling – she said, "I thought you personnel people were supposed to be nice." She had thought she was going to have a nice little informal drink.'

When planning your recruitment process, you may decide that an off-site interview is useful for a second round or later stage interview, but that your own premises are appropriate for an early-stage interview. In this case the chosen interview room should be smart but not too severe; boardrooms certainly can appear soulless and intimidating. It can be a good investment to select a particular meeting room as an interview location and ensure that it is always kept in a good state of decoration, with an atmosphere that encourages full and frank discussion. The room should be quiet and positioned so as to minimise distractions for both interviewer and candidate. Incoming telephone calls should be diverted elsewhere. Staff and colleagues should be asked not to interrupt for the duration of the interview.

The room's layout is also important. If an interviewer sits behind a desk, that can create an immediate barrier between him and the candidate. Instead, try arranging the seating so that chairs are positioned at approximate right angles each other; a head-on seating plan can appear confrontational.

4. Relax the interviewee

An interview is an inherently stressful situation. Most managers get stressed at having to interview people for jobs; for the interviewee the stress is many times worse.

Research shows there is nothing to be gained by artificially increasing the stress factor during the interview. Even if the position on offer is a stressful one, how a candidate handles interview stress does not necessarily indicate how he or she would cope in the job. There is nothing to be gained by deliberately upping the tension by aggressive questioning or other interview gimmicks.

In contrast, it is worth the interviewer putting in some effort to try and relax the candidate before firing the first questions. It should be your responsibility to establish rapport, not the candidate's. A friendly greeting is a good start. Small talk can also be used effectively to start building some rapport straight away. Rather than simply discussing the weather or local transport, try to personalise the initial chat. Most CVs will include a reference to the candidate's out of hours activities; this can provide an easy opener for discussion as you usher the interviewee to their seat. 'You are a singer, I see. Is that karaoke or choral?'

5. Ask effective questions

To get the information you need from candidates, you have to ask the right questions. Obvious. But not easy.

Too many interviewers see the interview as a form of conversation, but it certainly is not. An interview should be a structured mechanism for obtaining relevant information about past job performance.

Our recommended approach therefore is to use competency-based interviewing (CBI), also sometimes referred to as behavioural event interviewing (BEI). The CBI theory is based on the premise that past, recent performance is a good predictor of likely future performance. In other words, leopards do not change their spots.

Therefore, CBI seeks to uncover specific evidence of the candidate's behaviour in certain situations. How did this person handle the integration of the acquired subsidiary? What specific actions did he take to keep key personnel on board? How did he cope with the pressure to achieve rapid cost savings?

This is why planning before the interview is so important. Your focus needs to be on reassuring yourself that the individual candidate has the competencies required for the job. To do this, you need to have reviewed the candidate's CV in the light of the competencies identified in the candidate profile and job description. This should indicate key areas for examination during the interview. You can then drill down through these areas, seeking increasing levels of detail until you are satisfied that you have a real understanding of the candidate's actions in this particular situation. Remember that anyone can bluff in response to a question, but as repeated questions hone in on the issue in more and more detail, bluffing becomes increasingly hard to do successfully. We look at how to apply the CBI approach in more detail in the next chapter.

Within the CBI framework, try to use open questions starting with how, why or what. 'What skills do you have as a staff manager?' should provide more useful information than simply asking 'Are you good at managing staff?' You can also use phrases such as 'Tell me about ...' or 'Give me an example of ...'. These are extremely useful devices for getting the candidate talking about areas of experience that particularly interest you.

In general, you should try to avoid closed questions that require a yes or no answer; these will make it harder for the candidate to talk freely and harder for you to elicit the information you need. However, you do not have to avoid using closed questions all the time. They are sometimes highly appropriate, for example, if you want to check some factual information quickly.

Besides the kinds of questions you should try to use when interviewing, there are also certain types of questions you should try to avoid. These include:

Leading questions: This type of question telegraphs the expected answer. For example, 'Do you agree that passion for the business is an important characteristic of a team member?'

Loaded questions: Loaded questions invite candidates to choose between two given options, neither of which may actually reflect their own true opinion or action. For example, 'I presume you would expect someone to either put up or shut up?'

Multiple questions: Complex questions that seek answers to several points, or asking a series of rapid fire questions in one go, can obscure the real point at issue and leave both interviewer and interviewee frustrated. Keep your questions short and simple in the sense that each one contains a single query. Asking one question at a time will enable the candidate to answer far more effectively.

Hypothetical questions: Unless you are recruiting for particularly creative or analytical jobs, you should usually try to avoid hypothetical questions. In most cases the focus of your questioning should be designed to find out what the candidate has actually achieved in a real situation. Asking a hypothetical question allows the candidate to dodge this real life, behavioural aspect. For example, consider the scenario we use at the beginning of this chapter. How would you prepare for an interview? Ask any group of managers this question and the answer will include all the right stuff – reviewing the CV and the job specification, making notes and so on. Ask that same group of managers how they prepare in real life, and the honest answer will probably be completely different in most cases. Of course, candidates with any sense will make an effort to answer even behaviourally-focused questions with the textbook answers in the back of their minds. Even so, the responses should be more revealing, particularly if the interviewer persists with an issue and drills down to the detail.

6. *Encourage the candidate to talk*

Interviewers should never forget that it is the candidate who should be doing most of the talking. Unfortunately, untrained interviewers sometimes interpret a good interview in the same way that they would a good conversation. However, a good conversation implies 50:50 participation, whereas in an interview there is no way that interviewer and interviewee should be sharing the talking time equally. As a rough estimate, the interview candidate should be allowed to dominate by speaking for about 70–75% of the time.

Some people are natural talkers; others are not. People also react differently when nervous, as they are likely to be in an interview situation. Some candidates may be prone to prattle on, while others can become unusually tongue-tied. Whatever the situation, the interviewer needs to take control, being prepared to interrupt loquacious candidates and even resort to using some closed questions if basic, fast clarification of certain information is required.

In general though, the interviewer should encourage the candidate to talk. This can be done by means of verbal affirmation – mmm, yes, aha, go on – and by visual cues such as nodding of the head. If a candidate ends an answer when you feel there may be more to be said, rather than asking 'Anything else?', which invites a negative response, ask 'What else?', which implies that you expect more. Interviewers should also try to display positive body language, for example, avoiding crossed arms, frowning or looking bored.

Finally, do not be afraid of silence, which can be an extremely effective tool for finding out what candidates are really like and what they are actually thinking. Many people feel distinctly uncomfortable with silence and, in their desire to fill it in, will start revealing more than they intended.

7. *Be a conscious listener*

If the candidate is doing most of the talking, then the interviewer is clearly doing most of the listening. This is not a passive activity however. Effective listening is a complex business.

During an interview, the interviewer has to listen to responses with a view to finding evidence of suitability for the vacant position. You cannot just think, 'This is a good answer'. Is it a good answer in the context of the competencies you are looking for?

Effective listening also requires interviewers to make a conscious effort not to make snap decisions about whether they perceive this to be a good candidate or not. Factors such as appearance, the firmness of a handshake, the degree of eye contact, the confidence of a smile are all processed subconsciously and translated into: 'I like the look of this person' or alternatively, 'I do not think we are going to get on'.

Research has shown that untrained interviewers do not listen objectively; instead they often make up their minds about someone within a matter of minutes of meeting them. A survey conducted by Dedicated Research for Robert Half International looked at recruiting tendencies across six European countries. Its conclusions, based on 780 respondents, found that 40% of interviewers made up their minds about a candidate in less than 20 minutes, while nearly 20% had made up their minds in under 10 minutes. UK respondents were particularly premature in their decision-making, with 33% stating that they made up their minds within 10 minutes of meeting a candidate.

From that point on, without realising it, interviewers can start filtering whatever the candidate says to match their initial perception. If the candidate has made a positive first impression, then the interviewer is far more likely to pick up on all the positive content of the individual's answers and overlook factors which suggest they may not be suitable. However, if the candidate has been unlucky enough to make a poor first impression, perhaps simply due to nerves, then the negative content of his or her replies will make a big impact while positive content will pale in comparison. Interviewers must make an effort to avoid such pre-judgements. Otherwise they risk turning away talented people.

Secondly, at the same time as listening for evidence, the interviewer also has to keep in mind the direction of the questioning – what is the logical question that follows on from this response? If you are drilling down to home in on what the candidate really achieved in a certain situation and how they achieved it, you need to be able to think on the hoof. You cannot just work through a list of pre-prepared questions. You have to be able to adjust in the light of the answers, but there is a danger that the interviewer can become so focused on composing the next question that the candidate's response does not receive enough attention.

8. Note down key information

You may be interviewing 12 people at a first round stage, or just six people who have made it to a second-round short-list. Either way, that still amounts to a lot of information to remember about each one. If the interviewing process is to be successful, you do not just have to get the right information from the candidate; you also need to note it down effectively so that you can conduct a rational assessment of their suitability afterwards.

This means that during the interview you need to have pen and paper to hand. Jot down key points that will remind you of the evidence of suitability produced by the candidate. Do not write down verbatim everything the candidate says. For example, perhaps during the interview you explored why the candidate believed herself to be good at staff management, and she had explained how she had handled an under-performer on her team. Your notes could simply say: 'Staff management ability – handling under-performer'.

Once the interview is over you will need to write these notes up fairly swiftly so that you do not forget what your scribbles mean. Ideally, doing the write-up immediately after the interview reduces the chance of forgetting some relevant factor. It should not take more than 15 minutes. However, if pressure of other workloads does not permit this, writing up the notes at the end of the day before leaving the office will do. Try not to leave it any longer than that.

Last but not least, do not forget to tell the interviewee at the start that you will be taking notes. Explain that your note taking cannot be interpreted in either a positive or a negative way.

9. *Play the attraction game*

You will not be the only person making an assessment during the interview; remember that the candidate will also be assessing you as a representative of the organisation. You want to keep your options open as to whether this candidate comes to work with you or not. Do not forget the war for talent raging in the employment marketplace. If you think this person could add value to your business, some other employer probably does too.

Therefore, you must at all times treat candidates with professionalism and respect. Try not to keep them waiting in reception. Make sure they have all the information they need, both before attending the interview and at the end of it. During the interview, avoid challenging the candidate in a confrontational manner. You want the candidate to go away feeling that the interview was rigorous and thorough and that they were given every opportunity to present themselves favourably.

You must also do your bit to present a positive picture of the organisation, its culture, the team that the candidate may join and the vacant position. You want the candidate to leave with the impression that this is an organisation worth working for and a job worth doing.

Remember that the message you give about the organisation must be consistent with the messages given by other interviewers and everyone else the candidate encounters during the selection process. What impression are you trying to create? How are you describing the culture, the management style and all the other soft issues that create the working atmosphere? If the organisation is investing in developing an employer brand, the general message should already be clear. There should be no doubt about why you are an employer of choice. However, you will still need to discuss specific factors relevant to this job. Why do you think candidates should see it as an opportunity? Make sure everyone has the same understanding of the challenges and opportunities on offer. Contradictory information will put candidates off.

Bear in mind that candidates may not be looking for the same things as you, or indeed as each other. You cannot assume that they all want a company car or believe that work is the most important thing in life. Remember that Generations X and Y may have a very different outlook from someone in their early 40s. Try to understand what each particular candidate is seeking from their application.

However, while selling the opportunity, make sure you do not over-sell. First of all, if you appear to be pushing the positives too hard the candidate may feel naturally suspicious. Secondly, your aim should be to set realistic expectations about the position and what this individual's working life might be like if they join the company. One of the traditional problems of recruitment is that during the selection process organisations spend lots of time wooing candidates, telling them a good news story and creating an extremely positive image of life inside. Then, once the individual joins, all that attention is switched off. The new recruit finds that their expectations were raised too high and disillusionment can set in.

It is to be hoped that the position you are trying to fill is indeed an exciting one and that the organisation is a quality outfit. However, be realistic in the impression you give and avoid the implication that you are offering a little slice of heaven.

10. *Close the meeting professionally*

Once the candidate has been given the opportunity to ask a couple of their own questions, the interviewer should bring the meeting to a close. Thank the candidate for giving their time and explain what happens next. If this is a first-round interview, clarify when the candidate can expect to hear whether they are being invited back for a second interview. If the recruitment process involves tests, explain when these will take place and what they involve. If this was a final-round interview, give an indication of when a decision on the preferred candidate will be made. Be as specific as possible. Do not just say, 'We will get back to you in the next week or so.' Give an exact date. Assuming that you have been following advice in Chapter 7: The Recruitment Process, you should be working to a planned selection timetable and know when each stage of the recruitment process will be completed.

In general, you should avoid offering someone the job on the spot, although it is reasonable to give some indication of how you feel the interview has gone. If you have been impressed by the candidate, give them positive feedback. If you let them know they have performed well they should leave feeling favourably disposed towards the organisation.

Although you should try and avoid taking snap decisions about candidates during the interview, if you feel that a certain candidate does not in fact have all the requisite experience or competencies, then it is fair to give some indication of your reservations. It goes without saying that you should be diplomatic. For example: 'You clearly have some good experience, but some of the candidates I have seen to date have had more experience in the systems development area, which is a key aspect of this position.' A comment like this both gives praise and conveys the message that this candidate probably will not be your first choice. The candidate's expectations will already have been partially let down by the time a formal rejection comes through.

Remember that recruitment should never be seen as a static or one-off operation. You want to be constantly developing a talent pool. This person may or may not be right for the organisation now. But in two years' time? Make sure they leave the interview room with a strong impression that even if they do not get the job offer this time, they would be eager to apply again in future.

Panel interviews

In the private sector, most interviews will be conducted on a one-to-one basis. However, public sector recruitment makes far greater use of panel interviews. There are advantages to both alternatives.

One-to-one interviews enable the interviewer and candidate to develop a strong rapport because all attention is focused on just one other person. The interviewer has complete control and so can structure the interview exactly as he or she likes. There is less danger of another panel member moving on to a new topic prematurely, or of disorganised panellists jumping in and speaking over each other. Candidates may also feel less intimidated when faced with one interviewer, rather than a panel.

However, panel interviews can minimise the chance that a single person's prejudices will rule a promising candidate out of the running. They therefore smooth out the impact of individual bias. Having several people sitting in also reduces the pressure on the lone individual. As described above, the interview workload is a demanding one.

Probably for these reasons, evidence suggests that panel interviews tend to be useful predictors of successful candidates' behaviour. Dr Clive Fletcher says: 'Research indicates that if anything, panel interviews are slightly better at predicting performance than one-to-one interviews. Panel interviews allow for a kind of division of labour in the sense that while one interviewer is talking, another one is watching and listening. One of the problems with interviews is that the interviewer is subject to cognitive overload: you are trying to relate to what the candidate is saying, interpret it, use it to make some kind of assessment, maybe take a note of it and also think about how you are going to lead on from it. So it is very demanding to conduct an interview properly.'

In practice, many professional recruiters generally prefer to interview solo. If more opinion is desired, then a greater number of sequential interviews can achieve a similar effect, without cramping any particular interviewer's style.

Dr Gareth Jones, formerly Director of HR and Internal Communications at the BBC, prefers sequential interviews to panel sessions. He says: 'The panellists can start competing with each other to ask the smart arse questions. But I am a great believer in getting opinions from quite a lot of people. Sometimes I might say, 'Sarah, I think it would be great if you met the finance director because you would have to work closely with him'. The candidate can then have another set of conversations and you can get feedback. Sometimes people will comment on something that relates to a little tiny doubt you had in your own mind and you can go on and explore that further.'

Given the potential to use sequential interviewing to overcome any individual bias, one-to-one interviews are preferable; the advantages of openness and greater rapport offered by one-to-one interviews outweigh the advantages offered by panel interviews.

Managing panel interviews effectively

Panel interviews will need particularly strong planning, which means an even higher level of organisation.

Although some public sector organisations allow their selection panels to become ridiculously unwieldy, the maximum membership should be limited to five. Dr Fletcher says: 'Beyond five, it can be difficult to integrate the panellists. The interview will be fragmented and each person probably doesn't have sufficient time to ask questions. You also have a lot of voices chipping on the assessment. So going beyond five is not helpful and I would say that three is probably the optimum number.'

In the public and voluntary sectors, panels can often include politicians or trustees alongside the relevant executive managers. They may also contain some form of external assessor. Gary Hoyte, an HR Consultant and formerly HR Director of Scope, says: 'Employers might consider whether they could benefit from including an external assessor, for example, if you are hiring someone for a top role, such as the head of HR. Public or voluntary sector organisations sometimes borrow a head of HR from a neighbouring body, to help with the more technical aspects of the assessment.' In the private sector, you will need to find an assessor from a non-competing organisation, but this is possible. For example, when recruiting finance directors, companies sometimes make use of their auditors' expertise, rather than relying on the managing director to assess candidates' technical abilities.

Interview panels must be led by a clearly identified chairman who opens and closes the interview session. It must also be clear to all members of the panel how the decision on the preferred candidate will be made. Does the chairman have the ultimate decision-making power? Will the decision be taken by majority vote? Does any member have the power of veto? There is an inevitable danger that a group compromise may result in a decision that pleases no one, or that the ultimate decision-maker is forced to make an uncomfortable compromise.

The panel should ideally meet beforehand to prepare for the interview. It should be stressed to all panel members that they should not rely on others to do the necessary preparation. As part of the planning, the panel should discuss how they will co-ordinate their questions. In the public sector, where there is a particularly strong focus on equal opportunities, the panel generally agrees in advance a number of common core questions that will be asked of all candidates. However, some public sector organisations then think they cannot ask any individual questions, for fear that this impinges on the promotion of equal opportunities. Hamish Davidson, Head of the UK Executive Search and Selection Division at Pricewaterhouse-Coopers, disagrees: 'It is good practice to have a common spine of questions on key areas to be covered. Beyond that there are bound to be specific issues related to specific candidates that need to be challenged.'

At the beginning of the interview, the panel chairperson needs to make an effort to welcome the candidate and make them feel comfortable, or as comfortable as possible give the circumstances. Hamish Davidson suggests: 'I think the chair of the panel should go to collect the candidate and bring them back to the interview room, and then remember to introduce the other members of the panel. You should also make sure you have a fresh glass of water for candidates. In terms of seating, it's not a good idea to have a horseshoe formation with a chair set in the middle for the candidate, which can create a 'them and us' situation. You will get more out of candidates if you make the situation less confrontational.'

Some appointments panels may choose to open the interview session by asking candidates to give a short (10 minute) presentation on a pre-arranged topic (an idea we consider in Chapter 13: Testing Times). This can give the panel information on the candidate's presentation skills, as well as their ability to think on their feet when answering follow-up questions. If all candidates are given the same amount of advance warning (say a week's notice) then all should have the chance to present themselves in their best light. At the same time the recruiting organisation can benefit from some free consultancy by choosing a topic of current relevance to itself and to the role being filled.

Telephone interviews

Although not common, telephone interviewing can be helpful to an organisation that has received a large number of quality applications. Even after reviewing candidates' CVs or application forms, there may still be more suitable candidates than the recruiter really wants to interview face to face. Telephone interviews can be an efficient way of shortening the list.

Telephone interviews also have the advantage that they can eliminate some of the visual cues that influence an interviewer's likes or dislikes. Dr Clive Fletcher says: 'One of the reasons that some organisations have started telephone interviewing is to try and minimise some of the subjective impressions interviewers form. Telephone interviewing is increasingly popular at an early stage in the process, and the research shows that candidates' ethnic backgrounds have no impact on the outcome. There is not much impact related to regional accents either. There are some downsides in that some candidates find it off-putting to be doing an interview from home; they find it hard to psyche themselves up and get into the right frame of mind. People do actually need to achieve a certain level of arousal to perform well.'

If you do use telephone interviews, apply the same degree of professionalism as you would in a face-to-face interview. You should still follow the 10-point plan, although you will not need to worry about selecting an interview location. You will of course need to make sure you are phoning from a quiet location yourself where you will not be distracted.

In the next chapter we look in detail at how to ask effective questions using the CBI approach.

Chapter 12

Interviewing: Effective Questioning

In the last chapter we considered how to get the best from the interview by using our 10-point plan for interview effectiveness. In this chapter we consider the process of actually asking questions using a competency-based interviewing (CBI) approach.

Competency-based interviewing

CBI aims to uncover specific evidence of the candidate's behaviour in certain situations. It starts from the concept that if someone acts in a certain way in a past situation, the chances are they will act in a similar way if the same situation arises in future. With that concept in mind, the success of a CBI approach then depends on the interviewer drilling down to examine in detail the evidence that candidates give of their behaviour.

Drilling down

Conducting an interview is a bit like eating a sponge cake. A big one. This cake has lots of icing on top, with a thick filling of jam and cream between its sponge layers. To know what the cake really tastes like you do not have to eat it all, but you do have to take a bite through it from top to bottom. If you just nibble off the icing from the top, you will have a very poor idea of what that cake is like.

Some interviewers get stuck on the icing; they try to ask questions on so many areas that they get a superficial flavour of the candidate's real behavioural capabilities. A better approach is to focus on a small number of slices; drill down through a more limited number of topics in-depth – perhaps just three or four;

try to get to the bottom of the candidate in the sense that you find out exactly how she behaved in a particular situation, why, what the outcome was, how the organisations benefited, what she learnt from the experience, and so on.

Getting a reasonable flavour does not require you to talk through the candidate's whole career. Focus on the most recent work experiences. In general the further back in time you retreat, the less reliable the evidence on future performance potential.

CBI examples

When using the CBI approach, interviewers still need to 'funnel' down through the candidate's responses to get hold of detailed, relevant information about them. Your aim is to get the candidate talking about specific actions.

Too many interviewers seem to have a 'clipboard' approach to interviewing. They have their planned questions noted down. They ask each one, listen to the candidate's reply and then move straight on. This approach is not to be recommended.

Although we have said that the interview should not be seen as a conversation, since the interviewee should be doing most of the talking, there is one major similarity between an interview and a conversation in that the interviewer has to pick up on the candidate's responses. In a conversation, if your friend makes an interesting comment you do not usually ignore it, but respond to it. If they say they have just come back from a great weekend in Rome, you might ask: What did you do? What was the best bit? Why did you like that museum so much? Where was it? You get involved in sharing the experience. So it should be with the drill-down interview technique; you should follow up on the candidate's responses to funnel down to the heart of their experience.

A series of funnelling questions might go as follows:

Q1: What did you find difficult about your job at XYZ Plc?
Q2: In what ways were those elements particularly difficult?
Q3: Please describe a specific incidence in which you were involved.
Q4: What was your involvement?

Q5: What did you actually do?

Q6: What was the outcome?

Q7: How did you feel about the outcome?

Q8: What did you learn?

Q9: What would you do differently in future?

Obviously you need to adjust this structure in the light of the candidate's responses to pick up on particular issues you think most deserving of further expansion. Nor do you have to use all these questions if you feel you have learnt enough from the discussion on any particular point. You should never feel trapped inside a rigid interview format.

Within this book we have periodically referred to a fictional vacancy at an imaginary company, Best Books Plus. Imagine that Arthur Smith, who's CV we reviewed in Chapter 10: CVs and Application Forms, has now come in for an interview. When reviewing his CV, shown in Figure 10.1, the interviewer identified a number of areas for questioning. He decides to start the interview by looking for evidence that Arthur has a 'commercial approach' as specified in the candidate profile:

Interviewer: You say in your CV, Arthur, that as an active member of the Senior Management Team, you give commercial support and direction where necessary. What do you mean by 'commercial support'?

Arthur: I supervise the preparation of detailed management accounting information, and its analysis. I present this analysis to my fellow senior managers to help with commercial and strategic decisions.

Interviewer: Could you give me an example of the kind of decisions you have affected?

Arthur: Certainly. Six months ago we decided we needed to improve our efficiency levels. This was essential if we were to deliver the profitability improvement we had anticipated in our forecasts at the start of the year. I presented the Senior Management Team with an analysis of the impact of several different cost-saving alternatives, bearing in mind that certain cut-backs could impact our revenue growth potential.

Interviewer: What did you actually do?

Arthur: I recommended a particular course of action for improving efficiency. Although several members of the management team were initially opposed to my proposal, after reviewing my analysis for the different alternatives, we were able to agree unanimously on my proposal.

Interviewer: What was the outcome?

Arthur: In the first quarter after implementing my proposal we improved efficiency by 5%. This quarter we anticipate an 8% improvement.

Interviewer: How did you feel about the outcome?

Arthur: I was extremely pleased. My department, as well as myself, had shown our ability to shape the company's operating decisions. That's what I enjoy the most: being able to contribute to the future direction of the business.

Here is another example of how the 'funnelling' questioning structure might be used.

Interviewer: What is most difficult about your current role?

Candidate: I would have to say meeting the deadlines we are set by head office.

Interviewer: Why is that so difficult?

Candidate: The deadlines often seem unrealistic. Head office doesn't seem to take into account the staffing shortages we have had to cope with for the last six months.

Interviewer: Please tell me about one recent case of an unrealistic deadline.

Candidate: Well, we were asked to benchmark the performance of the Luton factory, using data compiled from other sites over the last year. The problem was, we were asked to make our report in three weeks. That didn't give us enough time to plan properly or to finish off our current work on the Birmingham plant.

Interviewer: What was your involvement?

Candidate: I was asked to head up the Luton benchmarking team.

Interviewer: What did you do then?

Candidate: First, I found out why the information was needed so fast. It turned out that the head of manufacturing had a good reason for his request, but I did manage to negotiate an extra week for our deadline. I then pulled together the team members and drew up a detailed schedule of work to ensure we would get the work done in time.

Interviewer: What was the outcome?

Candidate: We managed to get the work done fast enough to meet the deadline.

Interviewer: How did you feel about that?

Candidate:	I was naturally pleased and so was the head of manufacturing. Afterwards he admitted that he wasn't sure we could do it.
Interviewer:	Weren't you annoyed that he'd given you a deadline he didn't think you could meet?
Candidate:	Actually, it gave me greater confidence in my judgement; I'd known the original deadline was ridiculous, which is why I negotiated the extension.
Interview:	What did you learn?
Candidate:	To trust my own judgement, and to be prepared to challenge decisions or instructions that I think deserve questioning.
Interviewer:	Would you do anything differently in future?
Candidate:	Not in this case. However, since then I have pushed harder for an increase in the size of our department and I've volunteered to take charge of the recruitment process too. Having an extra person would have made a real difference in reducing the stress involved in the Luton project.

If ever a candidate gives an answer that you think seems inconsistent or vague, just hone in on the aspect that you want to clarify. Even CBI requires follow-up questioning to be effective. Dr Clive Fletcher, Managing Director of Personnel Assessment Ltd, and formerly Professor of Occupational Psychology at Goldsmiths' College, University of London, says: 'One problem with the competency or behavioural based interview is that candidates can start thinking up fictitious examples. Of course, it's always the case that with any self-report method of assessment (such as the interview) people can always lie to create a desired impression. It is up to the interviewer, even with a competency or behaviourally based interview, to probe and check to see if they really think this person has done what they say they have done. Have they really described what they themselves did, or rather what someone else has done?'

Interviewers' favourite questions

Inexperienced interviewers sometimes ask recruitment consultants for a list of questions they should ask candidates. Unfortunately, there is no magic list. As we have considered in this chapter, questions must be tailored around the specific circumstances of the job to be filled and the candidate in front of you. Questions must be designed to drill down through the layers of the individual's experiences to find out how they really felt and behaved, what they actually achieved themselves and how.

However, when researching our job-hunting guide, *Kickstart Your Career*, we surveyed a mixture of HR professionals, line managers and head-hunters and asked them about their favourite interview questions.[1] The results produced the following top 10 most *popular* questions:

1. What is the most difficult or challenging experience you have had to deal with?
2. What is your greatest career achievement?
3. What was your biggest mistake or disappointment?
4. Why do you think you are suited to this position?
5. What are your weaknesses?
6. What are your main strengths?
7. What are your ambitions: where will you be in five to 10 years' time?
8. How would your colleagues or boss describe you?
9. Why are you leaving your current job?
10. What do you like or dislike about your current job?

The top 10 favourite questions should be seen as offering an insight into the questions that other interviewers like to use. However, the fact that they are popular could reduce their effectiveness if candidates have prepared for them.

We asked Dr Clive Fletcher for his opinion of the value of such questions, based on his extensive experience and knowledge of the interviewing process. He says: 'There are whole books on '100 Top Interview Questions' or the like. The trouble with these, and with some of the 10 most popular identified here, is that lots of people are familiar with them and are prepared to give a set answer. This is not automatically a bad thing, but for some of the questions what you get is simply a piece of impression management. This applies especially to questions two, four and (to a lesser extent) seven above. Typical answers to number five include such classics as 'Oh, people say I work too hard', 'I suppose I am a bit of a perfectionist' and 'I don't suffer fools gladly'.

The main point about the questions is:

(a) they should be relevant to what you are trying to assess,
(b) they are followed up with adequate probing of the initial response.

Seeking behavioural evidence is much better than looking for attitudes or aspirations which cannot be verified and often have little or no relevance to how the individual will actually do the job. Asking people to assess themselves (as in some of these questions) is fine, but one should be aware of a large amount of research on self-assessment that shows it is subject to strong leniency and self-serving bias effects.'

What we did not ask in our Kickstart research was what questions these interviewers asked next. There is little doubt that, asked in isolation, this top 10 will not really help you get under the skin of your candidates. It is easy to fabricate an answer or waffle coherently in response to an initial question; it is not easy to keep it up in the face of a series of focused questions that drill down through successive levels of the candidate's experience to unearth what they really did/thought/ achieved.

If used in a real interview situation, the top 10 above should be seen as the top layer of the questioning cake. Sitting beneath each of these top layer questions are another six or seven follow-up questions. This top 10 would therefore become perhaps 80 questions in total.

The following example shows how the interviewer could funnel down from his starting question, one of the top 10 favourites:

Interviewer: What is the most challenging experience you have had to deal with?

Candidate: Well, so far that was probably when news broke that Fastbru was in talks with Quiksip Inc, the US company, and was possibly going to be acquired by it. As Northern regional manager at Fastbru, I had to explain to local staff what that might mean for them, and basically try and allay their concerns. The problem was that I didn't even know about the possible acquisition until the Sunday papers ran a story on it. Talks were at an early stage and only involved the main board directors. The news shouldn't have leaked out.

Interviewer: What did you do?

Candidate: First I had to verify the press reports with head office. I then had to communicate fast with our three northern sites. The managers there were worried about what they should do and say. Quiksip is a major player and our employees were understandably worried about what the takeover would mean for their jobs.

Interviewer: How did you deal with their concerns?

Candidate: Well, the first problem I had was to establish exactly what the implications were. Our head office said it was too early to tell. This made it hard to give the local staff the reassurances they wanted.

Interviewer: How did you deal with that?

Candidate: Well, I decided that honesty was the only policy. On the Monday morning after the news broke, I emailed the manager at each site a memo with information about the acquisition talks. I suggested what they might want to say and some answers to the questions I thought people might ask. For example, I thought people would ask whether some jobs could be lost if the deal went through, and I explained that we didn't know yet. In general I stressed that the talks were still in a relatively early stage.

Interviewer: What else did you do?

Candidate: I arranged to visit each northern regional site and held group meetings so people could ask me questions directly. I explained why Fastbru was considering the deal – that it could help fund new growth – but repeated that it was not yet certain the deal would go ahead.

Interviewer: What was the hardest part about those meetings?

Candidate: It was the lack of firm information. People were obviously unsettled but there was only so much I could tell them.

Interviewer: What did you do then?

Candidate: I told staff that they could contact me directly if they had concerns they wanted to discuss personally. I also told them that our local Intranet would be updated with any news if the talks progressed.

Interviewer: What was the outcome of those meetings?

Candidate: A few people did call me, and I talked to them to try to address their individual concerns, but most people seemed to accept that we all just had to wait and see.

Interviewer: How could you tell whether you were successful in your communication aims?

> Candidate: I had been worried that we would see an increase in staff turnover, which was bad news as our busy season was just coming up. As it happened, the rate of leavers actually fell. I think that's because I managed to convey a sense of the opportunities for growth that could result if the acquisition went through. I also think it was because I, and the site managers, made ourselves accessible and didn't try to fudge our answers. Our culture at Fastbru is an open one, and I think that really paid off on this occasion.

Interview expectations

Using the approach and techniques described in this and the preceding chapter should help you to get the best possible results from your interviews. However, using the interview alone as your sole selection technique will always have certain limitations. If you expect the interview to deliver conclusive evidence on all aspects of a candidate's potential job performance, you are likely to be disappointed.

Dr Clive Fletcher says: 'In the interview, you can only focus on a certain amount of areas unless the interview is to go on for a very long time. That means you need to focus on the things that are best assessed at an interview, such as evidence of achievements, drive, resilience, stability and some aspects of interpersonal ability. However, the interview is not the best setting to assess group interaction, for example; a group exercise is the best way to do that. An interview is not the best place to try and assess whether someone is a good communicator on paper. You should do that in a written exercise. The interview will give you a handle on how well someone thinks on their feet, but it will not give you a precise measure of someone's raw intellectual ability; that is best left to other methods. So belt and braces is the order of the day. Assessing people is a difficult process, and you need to use multiple methods to get the best results.'

In the next chapter, Testing Times, we consider some of the other assessment tools that recruiters can use to help identify the most appropriate candidate for the job in question.

Chapter 13

Testing Times

Recruitment is an inherently risky business, because until someone has actually worked for your organisation, it is extremely hard to tell how well they will perform in it. However, questionnaires, tests and simulated exercises provide extra information to feed into the decision process and so are a useful addition to the recruiter's armoury.

Why use tests

Tests, questionnaires and simulated exercises can improve the outcome of the recruitment process in a number of ways, including:

- providing extra information on candidates' suitability for the role in question;
- ensuring a fairer selection process, which will be respected by candidates;
- providing valuable information for use in planning the on-going development of the successful applicant.

Valuable extra information

The interview remains by far the most common method used for assessing a candidate's suitability for employment. However, as we consider in Chapter 11: Interviewing: Technique Tips, interviews can easily fail to deliver the kind of information that is really needed to make an effective recruitment decision.

Professional recruiters and HR academics believe that the more objective data and information you have on a candidate, the better. This is where tests can help. Dr Gareth Jones, formerly Director of HR and Internal Communications at the BBC, currently Managing Partner of Creative Management Associates and Visiting Professor at INSEAD, says: 'If you look at the history of recruitment there's been a search for the silver bullet, but there isn't one. I am a great believer in getting as much data as you can. I believe in getting information from formal settings, informal settings, group occasions, intensive individual occasions ... I am not against using psychometrics, although I only ever use ones that I fully understand myself.'

Chris Long, Partner in Senior Executive Search Consultancy Whitehead Mann GKR, says: 'For most senior level searches I always recommend that clients use some form of psycho-metrics, customised to the particular demands of the role, for the final shortlist or for the preferred candidate they are about to make an offer to. External recruitment has extra risks attached to it and you must do everything you can to minimise the risk.'

Fairer selection

Using appropriate tests, questionnaires and exercises should provide the recruiter with extra information on individual candidates' suitability for the vacant role. This can only enhance decision-making for the employer. However, there are also knock-on benefits in terms of the way that candidates see the recruitment process.

When employers use such forms of assessment, as long as these are accepted as fair and reasonable by job applicants, there is a positive impact on the employer's reputation, and the employer brand. All candidates are more likely to see the job as one worth having. Successful candidates will feel that, because they have proved themselves and been considered worthy, the employer is more likely to value them and take their on-going development seriously. Rejected candidates are more likely to feel that they at least had a fair crack at the whip but that in the end they simply lost out to a better applicant. Note that candidates should always be offered feedback on any tests and assessment exercises they have completed, as we consider later in this chapter.

Organisations that develop a reputation for using appropriate assessment methods, and for running demanding but fair selection processes, reap on-going benefits. Candidates may start to self-select: quality individuals will be attracted to apply, while weaker applicants may be deterred.

On-going development

Information gained from assessment activities can be used to plan training and development for the new recruit. This maximises the value to be gained from the assessments by maximising the individual's chances of performing effectively in the organisation.

Some recruitment experts actually feel that tests, questionnaires and exercises should only be used in the recruitment process if they are also used within the organisation for developmental purposes. 'It is less valid to use psychometrics in isolation, purely for recruitment, rather than also as part of management development and training,' says Ian Harvey, an independent executive search consultant. 'Assessment tools should really be used to determine candidates' development needs – to profile them; in practice they are often used badly – to find out what is 'wrong' with them.'

Types of tests

There are a range of different types of test that can be used in the selection process, including:

- psychometric tests focused on personality, which look at the character traits and behavioural style of applicants;
- psychometric tests focused on aptitude and ability;
- skills tests and business simulations;
- knowledge-based tests.

Personality questionnaires

These typically take the form of multiple-choice questions asking candidates about how they behave in certain situations, their beliefs and their attitudes or preferences. The results help the employer to build a picture of how the candidate relates to other people, how they deal with their own and other people's emotions, their motivations, working style and general outlook on life.

Personality questionnaires can be helpful in the selection process where the organisation has created a competency framework that identifies factors associated with success in the organisation, and then fed these through into the desired candidate profile for the vacancy. The candidate's personality profile can be compared to those characteristics to see how well suited the individual is for the particular role.

Personality questionnaires can themselves be followed up by an interview conducted by a trained psychologist. Such an interview may sometimes be used as a stand alone replacement for the personality questionnaire. This approach can provide in-depth insights, based on direct discussion, into the candidate's motivations, goals, approach to interacting with others and general management style. However, this kind of full psychologist interview is relatively uncommon practice, and is primarily used when making the most senior appointments, generally at board level.

Aptitude and ability tests

The terms 'aptitude test' and 'ability test' are often used interchangeably. (Note that experts in the field prefer the word 'assessment' as the word 'test' implies there is a right and a wrong answer; this is not the case with personality questionnaires, for example.) They are essentially focused on assessing the same thing – an individual's innate ability, potential to be trained or suitability for a role. One difference of emphasis is that while ability tests can be used quite generally, aptitude tests are often designed with particular jobs in mind.

Aptitude and ability tests can include:

- verbal reasoning – assessing the ability to understand, interpret and draw conclusions from oral and written language;
- numerical reasoning – focusing on the relationship between sets of data and measuring the ability to draw conclusions;
- spatial reasoning – concerning the visualisation of spatial relations between objects and pattern recognition.

The tests are generally conducted against the clock, so that candidates' speed of thought as well as accuracy comes under review. There are different types of marking system, the common one being a simple, straight addition of the correct answers. However, this means that candidates who are running out of time can guess at remaining answers (picking one of the multiple choice options at random) in the hope of gaining a few extra marks. Alternative marking systems can therefore be used to penalise incorrect answers and so reduce the benefits of making guesses. One option is simply to deduct a mark for each incorrect answer. Alternatively, the marking system could make proportionate reductions in the candidate's score, for example, deducting one mark for every three wrong answers.

Skills assessments and business simulations

These assess candidates' current levels of skills actually attained. Common forms include:

- in-tray exercises to test ability in prioritising key activities;
- presentations, either alone or as part of a group;
- other communication and literacy tests, such as group discussions or letter and memo writing exercises;
- role playing, to see candidates' behavioural styles in action;
- case study exercises, which can assess candidates' abilities in digesting information and suggesting appropriate actions or solutions.

Knowledge-based tests

Usually in the form of multiple-choice questions, these tests measure acquired knowledge. They are particularly common for testing IT knowledge, for example, to assess an individual's level of applied knowledge in a particular programming language. They can also be used to test applied expertise in using word-processing or spreadsheet packages.

Extent of use

According to the Chartered Institute of Personnel and Development's 2001 Recruitment survey, testing is fairly widespread in the recruitment process. The CPID found that:

- 60.1% of respondents use tests of specific skills;
- 54.5% use general ability tests;
- 44.6% use literacy or numeracy tests;
- 40.7% use personality questionnaires.

However, there were differences in the tests used for different types of recruits. The most widely used test for managers was found to be a personality questionnaire (used by 38.7%), followed by general ability tests (30.4%). For professional staff, recruiters prefer tests of specific skills (45.8%), followed by general ability tests (37.9%).

Assessment centres

Assessment centres provide an intensive selection environment, where candidates complete a bundle of tests and exercises tailored precisely to the role being filled. By trying to mirror the competencies associated with the position, they aim to give the recruiter the most complete information on candidates' suitability. They often include a combination of the tests referred to above, including personality questionnaires, in-tray exercises, presentations and case studies.

Assessment centres are generally designed to assess groups of candidates at the same time. This has the advantage of facilitating group exercises and being highly efficient for the recruiter. However, this also means they are less applicable for more senior candidates who will have greater concerns about maintaining confidentiality.

Dr Clive Fletcher, Managing Director of Personnel Assessment Ltd, and formerly Professor of Occupational Psychology at Goldsmiths' College, University of London says: 'A lot of people who claim to run assessment centres don't actually do so. They have just flung a number of testing procedures together in an ad hoc way without anybody being properly trained to do them. They would have been better off doing a competency based interview coupled with an intelligence test. Just because you call something an assessment centre, it doesn't mean it will be any good.'

Like everything else in selection, you get what you pay for. You need to structure the assessment centre properly, which means that you have done a careful analysis of the desired competencies, you relate the exercises to those competencies, you integrate the exercises and you train the assessors. If you do that, and spend a day or two assessing the candidates, then not surprisingly you get a better result than if you just spent an hour or two on it because you have a wider range of information. Assessment centres give you samples of behaviour, rather than signs of behaviour. If you interview people you get back a self-report and you are looking for indicators that they behave in a certain way; but in an assessment centre you actually see them behave. There may be a degree of artificiality and some limitations, but they do give some evidence on how people actually behave.'

Who to test

Tests can provide useful information for employers when recruiting for all types of role, including quite senior positions. However, professional recruiters suggest they may not be appropriate when filling the very top jobs, such as when recruiting chief executives for high profile organisations. Suitable applicants will generally have a high profile and strong reputation themselves. Their personal management styles and characteristics will probably be well known.

Furthermore, these positions are often filled with the help of headhunters, who will have amassed plentiful information on candidates by speaking to people in the industry about their performance, strengths and abilities. Independent executive search consultant Ian Harvey says: 'In a senior search assignment you build up so much research information on the person and on whether they are successful or not. It would, for example, be a joke to ask someone like Richard Branson to do a psychometric test.'

When to test

The most common approach is to use tests after the first interview when a short-list of candidates has been identified. The results of the tests can then be discussed at the next or final interview.

However, simple tests can also be used for pre-screening, an approach that becomes extremely efficient when combined with Internet capability and online applications. Mike Dodd,

Managing Director of Academy HR Services Group, which advises employers on recruitment and selection, advises: 'Say you are recruiting for call centres. There may be personality characteristics that determine a higher level of success in the job. If you can build a web-enabled questionnaire that effectively measures those characteristics, you can use that early in the selection process to get down to a core of suitable applicants quickly.'

How to use tests effectively

Tests do not provide a magic solution to the challenge of effective recruitment. Inappropriate tests that are poorly administered could even confuse the issue. Recruiters can maximise their chances that test results will be helpful by:

- ensuring the competency of test administrators:
- checking the reliability and validity of your tests;
- trying to minimise bias;
- relating the test to the job;
- not overlooking the value of simple tests;
- explaining the purpose and procedures involved to candidates;
- giving feedback (and a chance for comeback) to candidates;
- using test results for the induction and development of successful candidates.

Specialist testing organisations will be able to advise on how to select and run tests effectively. Recruitment consultancies, particularly top end search firms, should also have in-house occupational psychologists who can suggest an appropriate approach.

Testing competency

Testing must be taken seriously by recruiting organisations that decide to undertake it. Any kind of psychological test in particular should be treated as a matter for expert advice. Psychometric tests should only be administered by suitably qualified professionals.

The British Psychological Society has set competence standards for people wishing to administer and interpret certain tests. Level A covers basic psychometric principles and the skills required to interpret aptitude and ability tests, while Level B covers more advanced psychometric principles and the skills required to use personality questionnaires. Training and assessment by an appropriate chartered psychologist is required in order to gain the Level A and B Certificates of Competence. Test suppliers require anyone seeking to buy their tests to hold the Level A or B Certificate, as appropriate.

Checking reliability and validity

You need to ensure that the tests used are worthy of the purpose. Basic quality checks should include looking at the test's reliability and validity. Reliability is concerned with how precise or stable a test score is. This means that when you administer a test, you know how likely it is that the result is accurate. Validity is concerned with what the test score actually measures – whether it actually assesses what it was designed to assess. For example, if people score highly on extroversion, do they participate in group activities in ways associated with that trait, for example, by seeking out others, being sociable or acting in a spontaneous way?

When selecting a test you should check the extent of the research that has been done to back it up. Also confirm the availability of appropriate norm groups. For example, if you want to use the test on middle managers, you do not want to be interpreting their scores by comparison with norms based on school leavers.

Mike Dodd says: 'My key tip for employers is that they should double check that they are using the right test products. So many organisations use a limited portfolio of products that they seek to adapt to the role; instead, they should identify the key characteristics for success in the role and then select the product that will best measure that. Otherwise you may get an invalid measurement, which defeats the point of testing in the first place.'

One reason why employers sometimes get this wrong is because they limit themselves to using a single supplier of testing products. Mike Dodd explains: 'Many organisations have an obsession with using a single supplier. I can understand that they may have a natural reluctance to change; there are so many products and it's difficult to keep abreast of what's happening. But organisations need to invest time to make sure they are getting the best value for their selection process. Otherwise they may end up using irrelevant products and making costly recruitment mistakes.'

Minimising bias

A candidate's gender, ethnic background or social class may obscure or bias that person's true test score. This means that the test result may not give an accurate or valid indication of the candidate's ability, or their personality characteristics, in the area being tested. Test designers are aware of the issue and methods have been developed for evaluating whether a test score may be biased against certain groups. Employers should find out whether the particular tests they are considering for use in selection have been tested for such bias.

Some form of testing is widely used in public sector appointments once a short-list of candidates has been identified. However, there is awareness of the risk that personality tests, for example, may put candidates from certain groups at a disadvantage. Hamish Davidson, Head of the UK Executive Search and Selection Division at PricewaterhouseCoopers, says: 'Some parts of the public sector don't like such tests on the grounds that they discriminate by not taking into account diversity issues. There is a solid body of research to suggest that there are some discriminatory features in certain tests.'

Similarly, Davidson urges for consistency in approach if tests are to be used. He says: 'In ability tests, you often find that organisations assess both numerical and verbal reasoning, but not abstract reasoning. That's outrageous; many people think around problems and not through problems. So someone could score badly on numerical and on verbal reasoning, but actually be brilliant at abstract thought and at taking intellectual leaps.'

Relating the assessment to the job

Assessments are particularly instructive when they have a close relationship to the job in question. Therefore, business simulations can be extremely useful. If written ability is important, candidates could be asked to write a report. If research skills are important, get them to do some research. Such exercises can be based on real-life scenarios to combine a number of key skills, as well as intellectual ability. If the information is of interest and relevance to both the recruiting organisation and the candidates, so much the better.

For example, one banking group regularly recruited corporate finance professionals from the major accountancy firms. It decided to introduce a case study test to try and improve the predictive ability of its selection process in terms of actual job performance. The bank created a scenario where candidates were told that an important client – the chief executive of a major company – had just called to arrange an urgent lunch with the bank's head of corporate finance. However, the head would not be able to make it and the candidates were told they would have to stand in. The candidates were given a pack of information on the client and allowed a couple of hours to prepare before giving a presentation.

Feedback from the candidates showed that they thought the exercise sufficiently close to real-life situations and that they felt it was a fair measure of ability. The banking group found that recruiting people in this way did give a better indication of how people would actually perform in real life.

Simple tests can be good

If you decide to use testing as part of the selection process, you do not always have to use complex tests or questionnaires that require the input of a trained occupational psychologist. Simple exercises, closely related to the role being filled, can be extremely informative.

Chris Tanner, an independent business consultant and former director of training at Deloitte & Touche, gives the example of an organisation recruiting a finance director who will need to take charge of refinancing the business. Tanner says: 'As part of the selection process, when you are down to the last two candidates, you could try to get their ideas on refinancing. You could ask them to give presentations. People are generally happy to do this as long as you give them time to prepare.'

Sufficient explanation

Recruiters must ensure that they explain clearly to candidates what assessment methods will be used and what their aim is. This should include who will be told the results and how that information will be used.

Candidates must also be given clear explanations of the assessment process, including the nature of the exercise, the time available and how tests, exercises and questionnaires will be scored (for example, if wrong answers will attract negative marks).

Giving feedback

Candidates are most likely to see the assessment process as fair if they receive some feedback afterwards as to their performance. This may help them in future job applications should they be unsuccessful on this occasion; if they are successful, they can use the information to try and improve their performance as they proceed in the organisation.

Giving candidates a chance to explain the results of tests can also be valuable to both parties. It may be that a candidate had misinterpreted the aims of a test or not understood some practical aspect, such as the time available. When using assessment tools where there is no right or wrong answer – notably personality questionnaires – it can also be useful to explore whether the candidate believes the result gives a true representation of themselves, and if not, why not.

Some recruitment consultants will want to give candidates feedback on assessment results before they attend their final interview. However, giving candidates this information in *advance* is not likely to be in the employer's best interests. Mike Dodd says: 'By feeding back such information in advance of an interview you can prompt the individual to adapt their behaviours, based on the feedback. What you should always be seeking to do is to try and create an environment in which individuals display themselves in an open and honest way, which reflects the way they would operate in a particular situation. Otherwise, what you are doing is interfering in the assessment process.'

Induction and development

The results of assessments during the selection process can be used to help new joiners settle in effectively during their induction period, and to make sure the organisation gets the best out of them. Chris Long says: 'Not enough attention is generally paid to the way that psychometrics can feed into the induction or orientation process. For example, you might have a divisional MD going to join an executive team; the results could suggest how you can get the best out of that individual within the team.'

The tests may, for example, highlight areas where an individual might be helped by some rapid training to help them get up to speed fast. Using this knowledge effectively to tailor training programs increases the individual's chance of performing well, and quickly. This can be particularly important when recruiting in a tight labour market, where there is a skills shortage and employers may not be able to find enough people who already have all the skills they are looking for. Sesh Sukhdeo, Vice President, Europe, in competency testing specialist Qwiz, says: 'Testing can be useful to give an indication of how near to, or far from, the mark a candidate is. It can tell you what investment may be required to get them up to speed. Employers need to invest wisely in training and development, and using competency based assessment upfront can help give them a positive return on their investment.'

Graphology

For the sake of completeness we include a brief comment on graphology, which is used in some countries, notably France, as part of the assessment process. Graphologists claim to be able to spot personality traits from an analysis of handwriting. In the recruitment process, for example, this could be used to see whether someone is introverted or outgoing, and so on.

However, in the UK graphology is little used and little respected in terms of what it could add to the recruitment process.

Dr Clive Fletcher says: 'There is something in graphology, in that on the basis of people's handwriting you can identify broad characteristics, such as people who are highly introvert or people who are highly stressed. The trouble is, those kinds of judgements can be made quite easily without handwriting analysis. Also, these broad assessments can be made just as well by people who have not been trained in graphology as by people who have. When it comes to finer assessments, when you look at any decent research study of graphology, you find that they fail to show any predictive quality.'

Graphology brings little credibility to the recruitment party, so you may as well leave it out. If you rejected a candidate on the basis of an analysis of their handwriting, you would almost certainly find this a difficult position to defend in court because of the lack of credible supporting research.

Once all tests and interviews have been completed, the time comes to make an appointment decision. We look at how to go about this process in the next chapter.

The Final Selection

You have read a pile of CVs, you have run your tests, and you have grilled your short-listed candidates at a final interview. Now the time has come to pick your preferred future member of staff.

Reviewing recruitment aims

Once you are close to the end of the recruitment process, it is easy to forget what you were trying to do in the first place. Having sat through a series of interviews you may find yourself distracted by the promises candidates have made about their ability and potential, which may or may not be relevant to what you need.

Your first step in the final decision process should be to pull out the original job specification and candidate profile that was drawn up right at the start. Simply remind yourself of the competencies you were looking for in your desired recruit. Your aim now is to select the candidate who meets those competencies most closely. (If the final short-listed candidates have been not quite as impressive as you had hoped, you need to select the candidate who at least meets the essential requirements for the job.)

Pooling candidate information

By this stage you will have access to a significant amount of information on each of the short-listed candidates, including:

- applicants' CVs or application forms;
- any test results;
- any feedback from third parties (such as potential departmental colleagues, receptionists);

■ performance at interview;
■ references.

You should not overlook any of the above when making your appointment decision. Having met your short-listed candidates in person, their CVs or application forms may now appear irrelevant; but they can still serve as useful reminders of each individual's experience. If you have written notes on them, as you should have done when preparing for and during the interview, that should also jog your memory about any issues that concerned or impressed you.

Feedback from third parties should be seen as useful input to reassure you that a candidate you think is suitable does indeed have the necessary technical or interpersonal skills. Input from people the candidate would not necessarily have considered to be an assessor can be particularly informative. For example, how did the interviewee treat the receptionist or your PA? If they made a bad impression, perhaps this person is not as concerned with team spirit as they have claimed to be.

However, when making your final decision, most importance is usually placed on test results and interview performance. Test results should be relatively straightforward to interpret, assuming that they have been appropriate for the job in question. (See Chapter 13: Testing Times for further information on testing and interpretation.) Judging interview performance is potentially a more subjective issue, which we consider in more detail below.

As for contacting referees, most recruiters leave the checking of references until they have offered the job to the candidate and received an acceptance. We consider later in this chapter whether more effective use could be made of them earlier on.

Assessing candidates' interview performance

After meeting your short-listed candidates, one particular personality may leap out as being an outstanding individual, one you would love to have on your team. However, there will often be a number of people who appear equally suited to the job and deciding between them may not be easy.

Even if you feel instinctively that one person has outshone the rest, you still need to take time to review your notes and consider the factual evidence you have gathered against the job description and desired candidate profile. You should not get sidetracked into comparing one individual with another. Either this person fits the criteria, or she does not.

Remember that you are not looking for the 'best' candidate per se. You want to identify the candidate who is 'best for this job'. You do not want to offer the job to someone who is over-qualified, who may actually turn the job down or, if they accept, will come on board and quickly become disillusioned because the job does not challenge them as they had expected.

Your interview-based feedback on the candidate will have come partly from the answers given, and partly from the way in which those answers were given. This is all valid information for the decision process. Did the candidate listen to questions and give considered responses or did they jump in and miss the point?

Remember that issues such as the degree of eye contact maintained and the firmness of the handshake will indicate how much apparent confidence an individual has. But do not place too much emphasis on this if the position is not one that requires an individual to be out there leading a team. As we said in Chapter 11: Interviewing: Technique Tips, you must also be scrupulous in controlling your own prejudices. Because a candidate is overweight, that does not mean they are lazy.

However, you do not have to overlook gut feel altogether. If you are the line manager for the vacant position, you will need to work with the successful candidate. That does not mean they have to be like you (remember the classic mistake of recruiting in your own image), nor that you have to become best friends. However, the candidate will need to be able to work effectively within your existing team.

It is worth paying attention to whether the candidate's application makes sense in terms of their career to date. Do their current career aspirations seem reasonable and do they fit with the way the organisation sees its talent pool developing? Assess how motivated the candidate is to do this job well.

Finally, give credit to enthusiasm. When acclaimed British yachtsman Sir Chay Blyth is selecting paying customers to come aboard and join in his sailing challenges, he looks exclusively for enthusiasm and focuses on the underlying motivation for the adventure. When Ron Dennis, Head of the McLaren Racing Team, interviews a racing driver, he talks about one topic only: the driver's motivation.

References

References provide a useful, if under exploited, source of information on candidates. They can give you a first-hand account of how someone has performed in real life situations.

The best references are:

- from immediate managers;
- current;
- verbal;
- those that give personal opinions.

To make the most of references, recruiters should make sure that job applicants are not supplying names of friends or relatives, or even colleagues at the same level as themselves. Personnel departments are to be avoided if possible, since (apart from in the case of HR posts) they will have had little day-to-day contact with the candidate. The most appropriate referees are former bosses, preferably immediate line managers who will have had most managerial contact with them. The most recent bosses are most relevant.

Recruiters should try to contact referees by phone rather than seeking written reports. This is because people are generally more candid when giving their impressions during a conversation. The recruiter also has the opportunity to probe into any issues that are of particular concern.

Referees should be asked to confirm simple facts, such as the dates that the candidate was employed, their role or job title and the responsibilities they had. Recruiters should also ask for more personal comment on issues such as the candidate's strengths and weaknesses, the kind of working relationships he or she established, and the referee's assessment of the contribution the candidate made to the organisation.

Above all, try to get the referee's opinion of the candidate's suitability for the job on offer. This means you need to describe the job, including the key skills required, and ask to what extent the referee thinks the person's abilities match it. You should outline the key competencies required and get the referee's assessment of the candidate's suitability to perform well against those competencies. For example, if a key requirement is the ability to influence members of other departments, ask the referee specifically whether he or she thinks the candidate can do that well, and the reason for that opinion.

If you have been using a recruitment consultancy, you might want to ask it to take up your preferred candidate's references on your behalf. As we said in Chapter 8: Calling in the Cavalry: Recruitment Consultancies, there are certain advantages in using a consultant to do this. Consultants will have plenty of experience in the activity. They may also trigger a more responsive attitude, and obtain more insightful information, from the employer your new recruit is leaving behind.

When to take up references

In practice, offers are generally made to candidates 'subject to references'. Apart from habit, one key reason for this is often that the most significant referee will be the individual's current employer, someone the candidate will not want contacted unless they have an offer in the bag.

However, this will not be the case for other referees and the candidate may not object to references from past employers being taken up earlier on in the selection process. This may be a helpful option for recruiters having trouble drawing up a short-list for final interviews. Contacting referees at 'past' employers before the last interview may also provide useful information that can be discussed with the candidate.

Clearly, permission from candidates must always be sought before contacting any named referee, whether or not that occurs before or after a job offer is made. If a candidate does object to having referees contacted before you have made them a formal job offer, you must respect their wishes. They may have justifiable fears of being put in an embarrassing situation, particularly when they are working in a niche sector, or when the candidate is a senior person with a high profile. In such situations there may well be a danger of word of their potential job move spreading on the grapevine and reaching their current employer.

Legal issues

Although references can be extremely useful, some referees are cautious about what they say or write for fear of subsequent legal action. As an employer taking up a reference, you may subsequently be able to sue the referee if their information was incorrect. Such claims could potentially seek recompense for recruitment and legal costs incurred, as well as the salary paid to that individual.

For example, you receive a reference on a prospective employee – Jack Brown – from his current employer, Exco, that says Jack is 'honest, trustworthy and diligent'. You employ Jack, who subsequently defrauds you of £100,000. It transpires that Exco's files on Jack actually showed he had a criminal conviction. In this case you could well have a claim against Exco, since references must be honestly given and fair. Referees should always check their facts, including employment records, before giving the reference.

Employers who give you references, whether written or verbal, may well include a standard disclaimer such as 'This reference is given without any liability arising to us'. (This is sound legal advice for anyone giving a reference.) However, such a disclaimer may not necessarily guarantee protection from a liability claim if it is deemed unreasonable by the Courts.

Checking other details

Applicants lie on CVs. Not everyone, but a highly significant minority. People can be extremely successful and yet have fudged some of their past achievements, as the story of disgraced UK politician Jeffrey Archer shows. (Archer claimed to have attended Oxford University, naming Brasenose College in *Who's Who*. But according to his unauthorised biographer, Michael Crick, he actually attended the Oxford Department of Education.)

It is quite common for people to claim qualifications they do not have or to improve their degree result a notch. As an employer, if you want to be certain about the credentials of the person you are offering a job to, there is no alternative to checking on the validity of CV claims.

Areas for potential checking include:

- degrees and class of result;
- professional qualifications;
- key employment dates;
- the existence of County Court Judgements (relevant for bankruptcy or credit card problems);
- directorships held (and past disqualifications).

You can also check your candidate's name against the Employer's Mutual Protection Service (EMPS) database, which contains records of individuals dismissed for gross misconduct and operates on a subscription basis.

If this seems like too much effort, bear in mind the potential financial and publicity costs of employing someone who could potentially bring your organisation into disrepute. If you do not have the time to do the checks yourself, it is probably worth paying a specialist agency to do it. Charges can range from perhaps £10 for the most basic check to a couple of hundred pounds for the most detailed.

Health checks

Carrying out pre-employment health assessments can minimise the risk that a new employee will have an unknown, or known but undisclosed, health problem that impedes their future performance. If it turns out that the role in question is not appropriate for your preferred candidate, you can avoid making a recruitment mistake.

A selection checklist

This checklist may help you ensure you have considered all the relevant issues before taking the final decision. Consider what you know about your preferred candidate in relation to the following:

- work experience directly related to the role;
- professional and technical knowledge;
- demonstrable industry knowledge and experience;
- staff management ability;
- staff development ability (including coaching skills);
- evidence of past leadership;
- intellectual ability;
- communication skills (written and verbal);
- personality fit with the organisation's culture;
- ability to cope with/thrive on change;
- specific desired competencies (such as creativity, vision, detailed focus, etc.);
- potential for further development;
- enthusiasm for the role/organisation;
- motivation;
- third party endorsements (references);
- likely chance of acceptance;
- potential to agree appropriate pay and benefits.

If the recruitment process has been successful, one name should emerge as the most appropriate person for the job. Obviously the next step is to make this individual an offer, a process we consider in the next chapter. However, you still need to let the unsuccessful candidates know the outcome.

Giving bad news

At the end of the final interview you should have told all of the candidates as precisely as possible when they could expect to hear the result. You should try and stick to that timetable. However, from a practical point of view, you do not want to reject all your candidates until you have received a firm acceptance from your preferred choice. Therefore, you may want to delay contacting your second choice until you are certain that you will not be needing their services.

This delay can be problematic if your first choice asks for time to consider which will force you to break your agreement to contact the others. In such a case, if you are willing to give your first choice that time, you may want to go ahead and contact the other candidates anyway. Rather than simply rejecting your second choice, you could try and keep your options open to a certain extent by honestly explaining that you have offered the position to someone else. This can be phrased diplomatically. You should make it clear that you were extremely impressed with this candidate and that, if the offer you have already made is rejected, you would very much like this person to take the job.

'Look James, it's been an extremely tough decision for us. We really like your approach and think you've got lots to offer. We think you'd fit in brilliantly here. It's just that one other person had more proven team building experience, so we feel we must offer her the position. However, we have made it clear that we need a fast response and if she decides not to accept, we will offer the job to you immediately.'

Some people may, of course, decide that if they were not your number one choice then they do not want to be your choice at all. However, most people, assuming they were enthusiastic about the job in the first place, will appreciate your honesty and will be willing to hold their breath a little longer in the hope that they will receive that ultimate offer. Treating candidates honestly and openly, and particularly avoiding playing games with them, can only do the organisation's reputation good.

Closing the circle: reviewing the recruitment process

In the third and final section of this book we look at how organisations can maximise the results of their recruitment process by ensuring that new joiners start on the right foot. The way that you make your offer to your preferred candidate, and the way you handle their induction, are vital for on-going success.

However, we close Part II by highlighting the importance of reviewing the recruitment process just completed, and the value to be gained from identifying areas for improvement in future.

Feedback on the process can be usefully gained from a number of sources, including all those involved in running tests, interviewing, and even the candidates themselves. Suggested issues to consider are as follows:

The outcome

- How closely did the successful applicant meet the specified candidate profile?
- How many other applicants also met the key criteria?
- What plans has the organisation made to stay in contact with:
  (a) any preferred candidate who refused this job offer?
  (b) any well-qualified candidates who did not receive an offer for this job?
- Was an appointment made in the desired timescale?
- How has the employer brand been impacted by the recruitment process?

Value of the recruitment consultancy

- How good was the quality of the advice given by the recruitment consultancy on the most appropriate recruitment process?
- How relevant was that advice in retrospect?
- How closely did candidates referred by the consultancy as a result of an advertised selection process meet the specified criteria?
- How successful was the consultancy in identifying candidates as a result of a search (or headhunting) process?
- How well-briefed were candidates by the consultancy?
- What more could the consultancy have done to help?
- What more could the recruiting organisation have done to help the consultancy fulfil its brief more effectively? (This is a question to ask the consultancy itself.)
- How effective was the consultancy in obtaining and passing on feedback from candidates on the recruitment experience and the recruiting organisation?

Impact of advertising

- How appropriate was advice received from the advertising agency?
- Did the final advertisements reflect the culture of the organisation effectively and promote the employer brand?
- Did the advertisements attract enough attention in terms of candidate applications?
- What was the comparative success of advertisements placed in national and local press?

- Did you receive applications in response to advertisements placed on internet job sites or on your own corporate website?
- Were there any differences in the quality of candidates attracted by different sources?

Results of tests and interviews
- If any tests or assessment exercises were used, how did they deliver relevant information?
- How did that information add significantly to the selection process?
- Were interviewers satisfied that they managed to gain sufficient evidence about candidates' abilities from the interview?
- In what ways did the selection process address equal opportunity issues?
- What steps did interviewers take to attract applicants?
- Were the right people chosen to be 'selectors'?

Candidate impact
- Were all candidates given sufficient information on the job vacancy, the organisation itself and the selection process?
- How fair did candidates perceive the selection process to be?
- How much feedback were candidates given on their performance?
- How did the organisation try to promote itself and the opportunity?
- Did any final round candidates indicate that they would not want the job, and if so, why?
- What expectations were candidates given about the role, and were these reasonable?

Very few organisations take the trouble to seek feedback from candidates, even though this can provide a huge amount of useful information on how the recruitment process is perceived by those going though it. An easy way to get feedback is simply for interviewers, at the end of the interview and after responding to any candidate questions, to ask candidates a couple of quick questions on their experience. How useful did you find the information pack? What other information would have been useful to you? Did the tests seem reasonable? What is your impression of the organisation and how has it been affected during the process?

Of course, candidates may be wary of being too critical of the organisation before they know whether they are going to be offered a job or not. If more formal and detailed information is required, the HR department could always follow up with candidates afterwards by means of a short telephone interview or written questionnaire.

Given the pressure of workload faced by HR teams, conducting such research after each recruitment process is unlikely to be practically possible. However, a periodic survey of this type could provide valuable information that could improve recruitment results in future.

Items for improvement

Recruitment is a complex business and almost certainly there will be things that could have been done better. Conducting a review of the most recent exercise should generate a number of ideas for improving the process next time. These should be noted down straightaway so that they can be pulled immediately to hand when the next recruitment challenge arises. In the heat of a resignation moment it is all too easy to overlook vague good intentions that have not been formally noted.

In Part III we turn our attention to looking at how to make sure that your chosen candidate starts their new job full of enthusiasm – and stays that way. Recruitment cannot deliver its full potential unless employers focus on re-recruitment issues as well.

Part III

After Selection: Getting The Best From Recruits

Chapter 15

Making the Offer

The decision is taken. You have chosen your preferred candidate for the job. Now you have to make the offer.

Offer protocol

The general rule is, once you have made your choice, do not delay in making the offer. Your candidate may have been extremely keen to take the job when they came in for their final interview. But what if they have applied for several posts? If they are as good as you think they are, then other employers will probably want them too. Get your offer in before anyone else does.

When to make your offer

Best practice suggests that you should not get so carried away as to make your offer after just one interview, or even a second interview. Some public sector organisations have a tradition of making an offer on the spot, but this is only viable when all short-listed candidates have been interviewed one after the other. This approach also has the disadvantage of not allowing for much discussion or reflection about who is the most suitable candidate. As considered in the preceding chapter, you do not want to rush into a decision, but should go through all the information you have gathered on each candidate to make sure you are really assessing each one against the desired competencies identified in the job description and candidate profile.

Apart from rushing your own decision, making an offer at an early stage interview can actually put candidates off, particularly if this is a private sector appointment and they were not expecting it. Making an offer after just one interview could certainly arouse someone's suspicions. Why are you so keen to make an appointment? Are there not lots of other candidates lining up to take it? What is wrong with the organisation? Most candidates would expect to have at least two or three interviews, or meetings, with a potential employer before receiving a job offer. Acting in a way that contrasts with such expectations can simply put people off.

Of course, if your recruitment process has involved a greater number of interviews than normal, say four or so, then it may be more appropriate to make an offer at the final meeting. The candidate will have realised your serious interest in them by that stage and both the candidate and the organisation will clearly have had a fair amount of time to form their opinion of the other.

In general, however, if you believe one individual is an outstanding candidate you should make this clear at the end of the final interview. You should not be afraid to express your enthusiasm and even indicate that there is a good chance this person will receive an offer, but just hold back from going the whole way and doing it there and then. The decision to change employers is an important one for the candidate, and you should make it clear that the decision who to appoint is also an important one for you.

How to make your offer

Once you have allowed time for thought and have reached a rational decision as to your preferred candidate, the best approach is just to pick up the phone and call them. 'I'm extremely pleased to tell you Jack that we'd like to offer you the post of IT director.' Tell them that you would like to courier your formal written offer round to them straightaway. You can keep the call short and sweet, but make it clear that you are extremely pleased to be able to make the offer. A slight variation on this theme is to call and say, 'Jack, I'm delighted to tell you that we want to offer you the IT director post. How do you feel about coming in tomorrow for lunch and we can talk through the details then?'

Either way, you are showing that you consider this occasion sufficiently important to warrant the extra expense of a courier, or the celebration of a pleasant lunch. Such details may be small for the organisation, but can make a big impression on the individual receiving the offer. Compare this approach with simply receiving a letter in the post. How formal. How lacking in human contact. If someone is wavering between two potential job opportunities, small touches that make them feel involved in the organisation immediately can make all the difference.

Note that your offer should always be made 'subject to references'. We considered the process of taking up references in Chapter 14: The Final Decision.

Decision time for the candidate

When you phone up to tell your chosen candidate the good news, they may be so delighted that they accept there and then. However, you should not expect your applicant to give you a yes or no answer right away. Remember how big a decision this is. You only want them to say yes if they really want to come and work with you.

It is, however, quite reasonable to ask what their initial reaction is. You can also suggest a date when you need to know their decision. A week is a reasonable length of time to wait, but you should agree the particular day by when they need to tell you. Avoid general vagueness.

If a candidate tries to prevaricate you may have to say that the offer will be rescinded if you do not have a decision by the specified date. However, this can sound formal and unwelcoming, so you should try and avoid it if possible. You could explain that you are keen to make an appointment quickly. 'I have to say that you were head and shoulders above everyone else, Pete. And that's why I'm delighted to be offering you the job. But I do have another candidate who I know is keen to take the post and I need to let them know the situation soon. I do not mean to rush you, but I really do need to know what you think by next Tuesday.'

When making the initial offer, emphasise that you will be happy to talk over any uncertainties the candidate has about the job or the organisation. Make it clear that you are open to contact at any time. Perhaps the candidate would like to come back into the office and talk informally to some more potential colleagues? Would they like another tour? Would they like to meet up with the sales team?

Depending where the candidate's concerns or uncertainties lie, you may want to arrange a meeting with the HR department (perhaps to talk through issues such as the bonus scheme). Remain enthusiastic, giving signals that show you believe this is a good place to work and have nothing to hide.

Money matters

The offer you make includes two important elements: the job opportunity, and the financial package. If the candidate is to be persuaded to join your organisation, they need to be satisfied by the value of both elements.

By the time you make your job offer, you may or may not have established the remuneration expectations of your candidate, but negotiations are likely to be easier if both sides have a rough idea of the range in which the salary package will be set.

The easiest situations are those where the candidate responded to an advertised position which specified a salary band for the role. The actual deal will then depend on firstly, the recruiter's assessment of the level at which the successful applicant fits into that band, and secondly, the candidate accepting that assessment.

Even if no salary band was advertised, most candidates will probably have asked about the potential pay and benefits either over the phone before making a formal application, or at an early stage interview. Research for our jobhunter's guide *Kick-start Your Career* found that half of head-hunters and half of line managers felt it was appropriate to raise the subject of remuneration at a second interview.[1]

Establishing pay parameters

Industry norms are a useful starting point for getting an idea whether the package you want to pay is going to have a chance of attracting the quality of candidate you want. HR forums and reports by pay and benefits specialists can provide useful benchmarking information.

Potential constituent parts of the pay and benefits package could include:

- core salary;
- bonus;
- employer's pension contributions;
- share options;
- company car or car allowance;
- paid leave;
- private health insurance;
- subsidised gym membership and other benefits;
- reimbursement of home telephone costs and other expenses.

The offer will clearly need to fit within the organisation's own remuneration policies and guidelines. However, where possible such guidelines should be kept flexible. The more choice that potential employees have over the constituent parts of their pay and benefits packages, the better. For example, the more senior the position being filled, the greater the likely importance of non-salary items, such as pensions contributions and share options. However, a younger manager may be more concerned with the size of the monthly pay and the potential to drive a more expensive company car. As HR Consultant Stewart Rogers of The Rogers Partnership says: 'For senior people the maxim we often work with is that the salary pays the mortgage, the bonus pays for holidays and the stock options create the wealth.'

Flexible benefits

The spread of cafeteria-style benefits reflects the growing awareness amongst employers that employees like being able to choose between different pay and benefits categories. Equivalent staff can have the same value of benefits, but in a non-standard or unique mix. There is no downside for the employer, but significant upside for employees. Employers in a sense derive far greater value from flexible benefits packages because although the cost is no greater, employee satisfaction is significantly enhanced simply by virtue of being given choices.

Choice should not mean complexity, however. Packages should be interesting to candidates, offering them attractive rewards and sufficient choice, but they should not be unnecessarily complicated. Too much small print will cause headaches for employer and employee alike.

Adding a simple distinguishing factor to the organisation's pay and benefits policy, something that distinguishes you from close competitors, could also be worth considering. Chris Tanner, an independent business consultant and former director of training at Deloitte and Touche, advises: 'Be more distinctive. You have an opportunity to distinguish yourself from the competition. Find out what the opposition are doing and then see if you can improve on it. For example, if the industry norm is to give four weeks paid vacation, why not make your policy to give five or six? You can make yourself stand out in this way.'

Remuneration negotiations

Detailed negotiations will be left until after the actual job offer is made, when you have to clarify what pay and benefits are on the table. This is when the nitty-gritty of the package will be scrutinised by the candidate. If the candidate does not feel satisfied with the initial financial offer, negotiations may ensue. This is also the point when some degree of power has passed from the recruiter to the candidate; as the chosen one, the successful applicant may think it worth pushing for just a little bit extra.

As an employer, you should be prepared to show some flexibility. There should usually be some room for negotiation, influenced by industry norms, your organisation's own remuneration policies and the expectations of the candidate.

Terry Nolan, Senior Management Development manager at Unilever, says that employers need to react to the war for talent and be prepared to adjust their policies if they want to recruit the people most in demand. He says: 'We find that once you get above the median levels of income, pay negotiations do become very significant for top quality candidates. Whilst big companies need to maintain the rigour of their reward structures linked to organisation design, many other mechanisms are now common. Linking company value creation to individual wealth creation through stock plans is commonplace.'

Employers should not be put off by candidates who ask for an increase on the initial offer. People who move employers expect to receive a significant increase on the pay they are receiving in their current position. Professional recruiters usually assume that an individual moving jobs will be seeking a salary around 10% higher than they currently receive, while a salary uplift of around 25% is more the norm at senior levels. Research for *Kickstart Your Career* found that, on average, candidates were offered a salary increase of 9%. However, almost one in five recruiters said they would offer an increase of 15% or 20%.[2]

To assess how great an increase you are offering the candidate, you clearly need information on their current salary, including details of bonuses and options. Try to get as precise information as possible. For example, if you ask about the candidate's expected bonus this year, check what last year's actual bonus was and how it was calculated. Candidates may try and paint a slightly rosy picture to bump up their starting position in negotiations.

Candidates who do turn out to be hard-bargainers could be an asset to the organisation in the end. Ian Harvey, an independent executive search consultant, says: 'Many clients are perturbed if they go through a hard bargaining process. Things can get quite tough. However, they shouldn't be put off the individual. If someone negotiates hard with you, it suggests that once they are on board they will negotiate hard with other parties, such as suppliers, to your advantage.'

Special situations

In some cases employers may need to include a one-off payment to their preferred candidate as compensation for lost bonuses or share options resulting from the job move. Such one-off payments should be considered outside standard pay guidelines, since they have no on-going effect on the pay package.

A candidate who will need to move house may also ask for help with relocation costs, such as temporary rental accommodation. This may make relatively little difference to the organisation's bottom line, but could mean a lot to the candidate.

Timing of the candidate's move can also have an impact on salary negotiations. If a candidate is just coming up to the date of their annual review, they may expect a larger salary uplift to take into account an assumed pay rise had they stayed with their current employer. Rather than trying to second-guess what this rise might have been, the recruiter could offer to bring forward the candidate's pay review after they join. The starting salary could be agreed for the first six months, with the promise of an increase thereafter depending on perform-ance. Such a compromise reduces the recruiter's risk that they will be overpaying, while offering the candidate the promise of increased compensation in a shortened timeframe.

Involving a recruitment consultant

If the recruiting organisation has engaged a recruitment con-sultancy to help it find a suitable candidate, whether by search or selection means, the subject of the likely pay and benefits should have been discussed right at the beginning of the process.

'The head-hunter must be very clear, right from the outset, of the remuneration approach of the employer,' says HR Con-sultant Stewart Rogers. 'It is also important that the conver-sation between the head-hunter and the employer establishes the reality of the situation. Employers talk about policies and procedures, but the head-hunter needs to know the reality of what can be offered, the parameters in which they are working. What are the real restrictions on what they can or cannot do?'

The head-hunter will need to understand all the detail relating to the constituent parts of the offered package because candi-dates will inevitably want to know about them. For example, when will the stock options become available to the individual? Are there any contractual details that seek to tie the candidate in for a certain period of time?

Recruitment consultants can play a useful role as a broker between the employer and the preferred candidate. The con-sultant can establish what the candidate is looking for and try to shape the candidate's expectations, if necessary. The con-sultant should try to identify any potential deal-breakers early on and then see if these can be resolved.

After initial levels of interest and expectations have been established, the recruiting organisation may want to take over negotiations itself. The advantage of doing so is that the organisation retains direct control of the process. However, if there is likely to be hard bargaining, the employer may prefer the consultant to remain acting as the front man.

Negotiations can be particularly delicate with candidates who have been headhunted, as opposed to those who have been selected after applying for the post. Headhunted individuals will feel in a powerful position – 'If you want me, you have got to pay for me'. Given that this person may be perfectly content where they are, in a secure, well-paid position, the attitude is an understandable one.

Therefore, it is particularly important when negotiating with head-hunted candidates that employers have got the package right first time, and that it is without doubt an attractive one. Delay and inadequate offers can put candidates off, even if the final deal offered is a good one.

For example, one senior executive of a major retail operation received an approach to join a computer games company. The head-hunter put a lot of effort into courting the executive, who was interested in the opportunity, although he explained that he would not be willing to move without compensation for the stock options and bonus he would lose by leaving his current employer. The executive spelt out clearly the share participation he would require in the games company if he were to accept their offer. Unfortunately, the games company failed to take this information on board and made an inadequate initial offer. Although it did finally offer a package that met the executive's requirements, by that time he had lost respect for his suitors and decided to remain where he was.

Recruiters should take note of this story: if you want to attract someone senior and you approach them, you better make sure you get your pay and benefits package right first time, or pretty soon thereafter. When recruiting top people, you may not get a second chance.

Counter offers

During the negotiation process it may transpire that the candidate has received a counter offer from their current employer, intended to try and persuade them to stay. If that counter offer exceeds your offer, and if you want this candidate enough, then you may feel it worth equalling or bettering the sum.

However, each situation will inevitably be impacted by the rarity value of the individual in question; if there is another candidate who would equally fit the bill then you will not necessarily want to get drawn into a bidding war.

As part of your response to any counteroffer, you could try reminding the candidate of the reasons they have given for wanting the job with you: the new experiences, skills and challenges that you can offer. Few people change jobs simply to get more money; there are usual psychological and emotional issues as well. It may be simply that the candidate wants a change.

If you think that your preferred candidate is likely to receive a counter offer, you could even prepare them for this in advance and try to influence their reaction. There is nothing wrong with saying, 'You are clearly an asset to your company, so I have no doubt they will try to persuade you to stay. In fact I would be surprised if they do not offer you a rise. However, I hope you will not forget that we are on the verge of significant expansion here and there are great opportunities for the people managing that change. We would really like you to be a part of that success story.'

You might want to point out that when people do decide to stay with their current employer, most of them are looking to move again after a year. That is because the underlying reasons behind their original restlessness have not been resolved.

Contractual issues

After you have made your job offer to your preferred candidate, make sure they see a copy of the employment contract they will be required to sign on joining, or on successfully completing any probationary period. Showing them a sample contract before they start minimises the potential for disagreements later on.

Although contract details may have to be varied for extremely senior individuals with strong bargaining power, long fixed term or rolling contracts are to be avoided where possible. They have the same problems associated with them as do long notice periods, which we consider in Chapter 17: Re-recruitment. If an employee resigns it is difficult to stop them leaving after six months or so, even if the remaining contract term runs longer than that; if the employer wants the individual to leave earlier, it will need to compensate the individual accordingly.

Persuasive tactics

Money may be only part of the decision process for an undecided candidate. Perhaps they would like to delay the start-date in order to go on holiday with the family. Maybe they have been working on a flexitime scheme and are wondering whether they can continue to come into the office an hour early and leave an hour early. Perhaps the candidate is willing to accept a slightly lower salary increment in return for the anticipation of more interesting work or a more supportive environment.

Such issues are all potential negotiating points. You may decide to compromise on some areas but remain firm on others. The ultimate goal should be to achieve a package of pay and benefits that pleases the applicant but which fits in with the organisation's general remuneration strategy.

During the negotiation process your general tone should be one of willingness to compromise, with the assumption that both you and the candidate are seeking a reasonable and professional outcome.

Once your preferred candidate has been persuaded to accept your offer of employment, you still need to think about how to bring them on board effectively, a topic we consider in the next chapter.

Chapter 16

Effective On-boarding

O nce a preferred candidate has accepted the job offer, many employers just think, 'We've done it. Problem solved. Recruitment project over.'

But they'd be wrong. The more effort employers put into helping their new star player feel a part of the organisation – even before the new joiner officially starts working there – the better.

That insider feeling

The more someone feels *involved* with an organisation, the more likely they are to enjoy working there, the better they are likely to perform and the longer they are likely to stay. So encouraging your new recruit to feel at home is an extremely important part of the recruitment process.

You can start helping new recruits to develop that 'insider' feeling right from the moment they accept your job offer. In fact, you should even have started before that, by treating candidates with friendliness and respect and responding openly to any questions they have about the organisation or the job.

However, the serious relationship building really starts once someone has agreed to join you. Or at least it should. The problem is, the new joiner will probably have to complete a notice period with their current employer. That means there could be a delay of a month, three months, six months or occasionally even longer before they walk through your doors as an actively participating member of your team (although overly long notice periods are frowned upon by the Courts and can be reduced, as we note in Chapter 17: Re-recruitment).

During this delay both joiner and employer can easily take each other for granted. By the time the start date arrives some of that mutual excitement at a deal well done and the opportunities ahead may well have dissipated.

Therefore, the recruiting organisation needs to make an effort not only to stay in contact with the new joiner during the pre-start period, but also to start involving them in the organisation's affairs. Activity designed to engender a feeling of inclusiveness could take the form of:

- inviting the new recruit to occasional staff social activities;
- arranging meetings between the joiner and current team members;
- including the joiner on the staff newsletter mailing list;
- sending through copies of recent newsletters and organisational reports or announcements;
- planning ahead any immediate training needs;
- briefing the new recruit on your organisation's induction procedures.

Effective induction

The purpose of an induction process, or 'on-boarding' as the Americans call it, should be to welcome a new employee, help them feel at home in the organisation and get them up to speed with what their role involves. Induction is all about orientation – helping the new joiner feel they belong, and fast.

This sounds simple, but many organisations are dreadfully poor at it, apart from when managing bulk intakes, usually of new graduates, who all join on the same set dates. It is a very different matter, however, when a single middle manager turns up one day in the middle of June just a week before the Annual General Meeting.

Even basic induction practices can easily be overlooked. For example, new joiners have been known to turn up on their start date, full of enthusiasm, only to find that their line manager is on holiday, no one in their department knew they were coming and there is not even a chair for them to sit on. What kind of impression does this make? If the new joiner had any expectations at all of the employer, these will have been well and truly ruined within the first hour of their first day. Similarly, senior hires may often be left to their own devices because people assume they have seen it all before. Well, they may have done; but not in your organisation.

Induction processes can fail to deliver in other ways too. Some organisations, for example, offer periodic induction sessions to groups of recruits on set dates. But if you happen to join on May 15 and the next induction date is not until July 30, the session will not be much use to you.

Successful induction takes time and commitment from HR and from line managers. Unfortunately there are no shortcuts. Recommended practice for maximising the chances for a successful induction includes:

- planning what will happen when;
- meeting any immediate training requirements;
- giving each new joiner a 'buddy' or 'partner';
- ensuring new joiners have the information they need;
- setting up induction projects.

Effective planning

You need to know exactly what will be done to help the new joiner settle in during their first day, first week and on into the first few months. This should include:

- who greets the individual;
- where they will sit (assuming it is not a hot-desking office);
- who will brief them on departmental practices and processes;
- what training will be available and when;
- what work they will be given;
- how their progress will be monitored;
- what the key priorities are for the new joiner, such as specific objectives and early deadlines.

You should also identify an appropriate existing member of staff to take part in a 'partner programme' or a 'buddy system'.

Training needs

As we considered in Chapter 13: Testing Times, the use of additional selection methods such as psychometric or other tests can enhance the process of choosing the most appropriate candidate. However, such tests should not be used in isolation, but linked to the on-going training and development plan for the successful candidate.

The induction period is the key time for clarifying what training the new joiner needs immediately, to help them get up to speed fast, and what they may subsequently require to maintain their developmental momentum. Such an approach not only increases the likelihood that the chosen candidate will actually perform as well as expected, it also reinforces the new joiner's positive impression of the organisation and helps to engender a degree of commitment to it. This is all part of the general best practice aim to create a strong employer brand.

Buddies

No one doubts that the first few days, even weeks, in a new organisation can be confusing. There is a huge amount to take in at once – names of colleagues, departmental locations, office practices, computer passwords, how IT systems work, what needs to be done when. Even if someone is given an office tour during the recruitment process and again on the day they join, that does not mean they can be expected to know from then on exactly what happens where.

Much of the stress of settling in can be eased by allocating the new joiner a 'buddy' or 'partner' who they can approach for help and advice as and when they need it. This kind of approach has been adopted by companies such as General Electric, Microsoft, Dell, IBM and Robert Half International. The buddy could be a colleague doing a similar job in the same department or, for senior managers, someone of equivalent status in another department. The buddy could be paid a bonus to reflect the importance of the role and the fact that it will take up time in addition to the individual's normal job; at Robert Half International buddies received bonuses of around two days' salary for each month of the induction process.

The buddy undertakes to help the new joiner for the duration of the induction, which may be 30, 60 or 90 days, as deemed appropriate. During this period the buddy can get together with the new joiner at agreed times – perhaps initially for half an hour each week – to talk over any concerns. Outside those meetings, the new joiner should feel free to contact the buddy at any time to ask for immediate advice if their line manager is not around to help. It should be clear, however, that the prime responsibility for ensuring that the new joiner enjoys a successful induction rests with the immediate line manager.

Key information

A basic but essential element in successful induction is making sure the new joiner has access to plentiful information about the organisation, their department and role. Buddies play a major part in this, but simply providing a joiner information pack can also be a major help. The pack could include:

- an organisational diagram;
- names and titles of key people (from departmental heads to receptionists);
- a brief history of the organisation's development;
- key client details;
- key operational procedures (such as how to book meetings rooms, how to report computer faults);
- information on all in-house facilities;
- an internal phone directory.

The new joiner may already have some of this information if the employer has made an effort to familiarise them with the organisation during the pre-start period. Even so, having a pack presented to you on the first day suggests an on-going willingness to help the new team member settle in.

However, new joiners should not be made to feel that the pack contains everything they need to know; they should be encouraged to ask questions of colleagues, their line manager and their buddy as and when they need. Nor should the new joiner be given the impression that the information they are given, for example on procedures or systems, can never be challenged. Your new employee may have some useful insights on how things could be done better.

Induction projects

Organisations can make use of the fresh eyes and ears of new recruits far more effectively than they do, as Chris Tanner, an independent business consultant and former director of training at Deloitte & Touche, points out. He says: 'Someone coming into the organisation, who has no historical or political baggage, can offer a fresh opinion; they *can* see the wood for the trees. We should use the benefit of those first impressions by getting them to conduct a meaningful, well-defined project during perhaps the first three months. They could review existing processes (including the recruitment process itself), procedures and systems, examine current ways of doing things. Rather than telling them, 'This is the way we do things here', ask them to have a look and see what they think. Organisations that have tried this have found the results extremely useful. Plus, the approach means that the person coming in feels empowered to ask lots of questions. It is made clear to everyone that they are working on this project. So they meet a lot of people, which helps them settle in, and at the same time they have a valuable role that can add value to the organisation straight away.'

New employees are also useful sources of information on the organisation's recruitment process. In Chapter 14: The Final Selection, we considered the value of seeking feedback from candidates on how they perceived the experience. Your new recruit is the most accessible of the candidates and so, during the induction process, it would be worth asking specific questions about each stage – advertising, applications handling, testing and interviewing. You could learn about areas needing improvement.

You can seek feedback again at the end of the induction process, or perhaps three months after the individual's start-date. Questions to ask could include:

- Did the joiner's experiences in the first weeks and months match their expectations?
- Did they feel let down in anyway?
- How useful was the induction process?
- How could it be improved?
- How quickly did they feel part of the team?

Unilever has recognised the vital role that induction can play in helping new executive hires to settle in and has now developed a model on-boarding plan for use globally. Prior to that, a small internal survey found that it took an average of three months for people to feel comfortable in Unilever, and sometimes as long as six or nine months. The speed with which people felt comfortable had a direct correlation with the quality of their induction.

Terry Nolan, Senior Management Development Manager at Unilever, says: 'If you bring someone in at a reasonably senior level, be aware that they need a lot of love and attention to get them into the business. They probably need a lot of heavy attention on three dimensions: first, how they inform themselves about the business, the data, the process flows; secondly, how they are to measure themselves or how they will be measured – that's the expected output; and thirdly, how do they behave themselves – which behaviours will allow them to be successful in their new environment?'

Unilever's global on-boarding model now sets out recommended practices pre-arrival, in the new hire's first 30 days, and then for regular periods thereafter. For example, in the pre-arrival period arrangements are made for the new hire to come in and go through the induction plan. In the first 30 days the model calls for extensive staff introductions, meetings with peers and team members as well as the development of an individual on-boarding plan, including objectives to be met by the 100th day of employment. These cover issues around the organisational structure and culture, the individual's role and responsibilities and personal development. The new hire is also introduced to an internal mentor.

Another European blue-chip company has also redesigned its induction process to ensure that employees settle in fast and start identifying with the organisation, and working productively, fast. Key elements of the induction process can be summarised as

- starting the process at, or before, the signing of the contract;
- ensuring ownership (allocated responsibility) for the induction process;
- appointing coaches (internal and external);
- ensuring the first week is special;
- establishing 100-day objectives;
- balancing information-giving versus discovery;
- ensuring the new entrant has tools and support to concentrate on their real job;
- facilitating networking;
- providing feedback.

Probationary periods

Requiring new joiners to complete a probationary period before they are offered a firm contract provides a degree of comfort for the employer. If, despite the recruiter's best effort, the new joiner proves unsuitable for the role, their contracts can be terminated very easily.

Extent of use

Jonathan Ebsworth, partner in solicitors Reid Minty, says: 'For all but senior level appointments, an employer should not sign an employment contract without a probationary period. That's because you can never know absolutely who, or what, you are getting. Someone may come over well at interview, but have serious personal problems – be an alcoholic, for example, or have not been honest in their CV. So as an employer it's sensible to use probationary periods as a matter of policy.'

The main hitch in this approach may occur when hiring senior personnel who are essentially moving from one top-level post to a similar one. They are unlikely to agree to any probationary element because they will have too much to lose in leaving a secure post for an uncertain one.

Negotiating chips

Even for lower level posts, preferred candidates may object to having to complete a probationary period. In this case the recruiting organisation will have to argue its case. This will be made easier if you can show that the policy is generally accepted in the organisation, for example, that all the existing directors completed a probationary period and none were sacked as a result. If you can demonstrate a strong induction process, with extensive support being made available to new joiners, that may also help to persuade candidates that the probationary terms are reasonable and are for the protection of everyone in the organisation.

You could also negotiate on the terms of the probation and the way that it impacts on benefits. Jonathan Ebsworth says: 'Sometimes employers only start paying pension contributions once the probationary period is over. In this case you could offer to backdate the contributions as a sweetener. This may help you to persuade the individual to accept the probation and leave them with the impression that it is fair.'

Effective management

If an organisation is to make use of probationary periods, it must ensure that it manages the process properly. First of all, the new joiner must understand exactly what will be required of them if they are to meet the required standard. Secondly, the organisation must establish exactly how that standard is to be measured and by whom. The new joiner must be given regular feedback, particularly if their performance seems to be going off track. Their line manager must be prepared to explain to them what they are doing inadequately, and be willing to spend time coaching them towards improvement.

The HR department will need to ensure that the new joiner is receiving the monitoring and guidance necessary and will need to keep in regular contact with the line manager. Shortly before the end of the probationary period – say after two out of three months' probation – HR should phone or e-mail the line manager to remind them that they will need to take a decision on their new recruit in the near future.

You do not want to find that the line manager forgets about the probationary requirement. It has been known for organisations to let the end of the probation to slip past unnoticed. Then, two weeks too late, the line manager calls up HR and says, 'I don't think this person is up to the job. We've got to replace them.' At that point the procedure for ending the contract becomes less straightforward.

When the end of the probation arrives, the organisation has three choices in the news, it gives the new joiner:

- Congratulations! You have passed with flying colours and we are happy to say you are now on a normal full contract; or
- I am afraid, as you know from previous feedback, you have not managed to reach the standard we were expecting. I am sorry that we cannot keep you on here; or
- Well, I know you have been struggling a bit, but you have been improving. So we are going to extend your probationary

period for another three months. If you keep on improving, I am confident we can put you on a full contract at the end of that time.

If the recruitment process was handled effectively, the chances are that the probationary period will have proved unnecessary; your new joiner will have settled in fast and be on the way to becoming a high performer in your organisation. The employer's primary concern then will be to build on that promising start to help achieve a value-adding relationship with the employee for as long as both parties benefit, an issue we consider in the next chapter.

Chapter 17

Re-recruitment

The recruitment process has to be seen as part of the long-term seduction of the individual employee. Someone will take a decision to join an organisation once; they then take the decision to stay every day thereafter. Employers need to commit to the re-recruitment of their staff on an on-going basis. This is the best way to satisfy the personal demands of the workforce as well as the strategic aims of the organisation.

After induction and probation

In the previous chapter we considered the vital importance of the induction process for helping an employee to settle in. Just because a new joiner's induction and probationary periods are over, that does not mean the recruiting organisation can sit back, relax and look forward to years of productive activity from their new recruit. The organisation needs to make an on-going commitment to developing their new joiner.

A Universum survey of graduates with eight years work experience highlighted the importance of continuing to offer training and development experiences to employees. Asked what would encourage their loyalty to an employer, 57% of women and 51% of men cited opportunities for professional training and development.[1] This attracted more support from both genders than did promotional opportunities or generous salaries and benefits.

Training and development

A large part of this development process will require the provision of appropriate training, as well as coaching or mentoring. Training has a valuable part to play in helping employees feel they are progressing professionally and personally. But that training needs to be appropriate to individual needs, deemed valuable by line managers and delivered at the time and in the manner that the individual needs it. New skills acquired through training also need to be reinforced quickly in real life situations. For example, line managers should get involved soon after team members have completed any training exercises to encourage and support them to use their new skills or methods in real life in the job.

Because of the variable results, traditional classroom-based training is increasingly being supplemented by online courses delivered via the Internet, or the organisation's own intranet, that can let people develop their skills as and when it suits them. In addition, there is increasing evidence that effective mentoring or coaching is the major determinant in encouraging an individual to perform to their best ability.

Mentoring and coaching

Mentoring enables the individual to talk through issues that challenge them, whether related to the operations of the organisation itself or to their own personal strengths and weaknesses. Discussions with a more senior, respected individual, but not someone to whom they normally report directly, can provide a valuable, impartial sounding board and a source of support and advice as the individual progresses in the organisation.

Coaching can provide similar support, but this time from the individual's line manager. Coaching theory recognises that people learn in different ways, but that they generally learn most effectively from their own experience. It therefore requires line managers to spend time encouraging, motivating or instructing their staff as they do their work.

Depending on the personalities involved, the coaching style may be gently encouraging and designed to boost confidence; or it may be more assertive and designed to shake up someone who has become complacent about their work. The coaching style should be determined by the character and needs of the individual being coached, not the personality of the coach. Former England football coach Terry Venables is widely considered to have been an excellent coach – willing to give some people a kick up the backside and others an arm round the shoulder, whatever that particular person needed to get them back on peak form.

Coaching is itself a major skill, and one that managers will themselves need to be trained and coached in. However, if a coaching mentality becomes the norm, the effects on staff morale, team performance and the organisation's general success can be significant.

Appraisals

Alongside mentoring and coaching, appraisals offer a more formal vehicle for providing feedback to individual staff members on their performance over a given period. However, their effectiveness is generally limited by their infrequency; many organisations have annual appraisal systems, which means that long periods of time can elapse between some particular action, or piece of work, by the staff member concerned and the feedback given on it. This does no one much good, and so we recommend that appraisals be conducted at least biannually and preferably on a quarterly basis.

To be most effective, the appraisal should be handled by the immediate line manager who has intimate knowledge of the individual's achievements. There needs to be genuine commitment to drawing up and delivering an action plan to help the individual perform even better in future. Both the line manager and the person to be appraised should have enough advance warning to be able to prepare effectively and think through issues they want to raise. Topics for discussion could include:

- how the individual feels about their role;
- particular areas where there is room for improvement;
- the training or coaching needed to help achieve that improvement;
- how the improvement can be measured;
- plans for career development in the next year and perhaps looking ahead two or three years.

There should also be continuity between appraisals, so that goals set in the previous appraisal can be discussed. How successfully were they achieved? If not very successfully, why not?

The discussion should aim to be constructive rather than acrimonious and within the context of being a 'learning organisation'. The organisation, and all those in it, should benefit from the sense that there is on-going support for development and improvement, at all levels. However, you should not shy away from problems that may exist with a particular employee; the appraisal provides an appropriate forum for such a discussion and also enables you to put on record any such problems for future reference. You might make use of such notes, for example, should you in future decide to fire someone who has statutory protection under the UK's unfair dismissal legislation. We consider such issues in Chapter 18: Firing. You should make sure, of course, that you give the employee a genuine opportunity to air any grievances too.

The need for re-recruitment

The decision to work for an employer is a complex one. People decide to join an organisation for a variety of reasons, which often include some or all of the following:

- This organisation's culture and values fit with my own.
- I feel I will get on with the people there.
- I feel I will belong there.
- I believe in the quality of this organisation's products or services.
- I will receive training and development opportunities.
- I will be paid the salary I think I deserve.
- I will be able to work on projects/issues/areas that matter to me.
- This organisation has a good reputation for treating staff well.

Over time, an individual's personal career aims or attitudes may change. The kind of projects that interest them may alter, or they may need to move locations for family reasons. In such cases, there is probably little the organisation can do to prevent the employee leaving. However, if the employee resigns because the organisation no longer meets their expectations in ways that it should or could, this is a failure on the employer's part.

If an organisation wants to retain employees for as long as both parties are adding value to the other, then it needs to try and meet each employee's expectations as far as it can. This means the organisation must deliver on its recruitment promise and remain true to its employer brand. The employer must continually provide evidence – through its culture, its development system and its responsiveness to individual needs – that the employee is working in the right environment. In essence, employers need to be constantly re-recruiting their existing workforce.

Understanding employees' needs

As we said in Chapter 3: Strategies for Successful Recruitment, any organisation needs to have an understanding of why its employees choose to work there, why they stay and why they leave. This information helps to shape the conscious understanding of an employer brand.

You can keep up-to-date with employees' opinions by asking joiners why they join. This can be handled in the post-recruitment review phase, as described in Chapter 14: The Final Selection.

You can also seek the opinions of current employees as to why they stay. This information can be gained by pooling feedback from annual reviews or mentoring sessions about what individuals have recently gained from their working life. Another approach is to use anonymous attitude surveys. Conducting such research on an annual basis can give you a useful snapshot of how people are feeling and how effective new employment policies have been; it can also help to identify any new issues of concern that HR and the management team should know about.

Sometimes the results of surveys deliver unexpected results. Robert Half International conducted a survey of its employees to ask them why they stayed with the organisation; some employees had been with the company for an unusually long time when compared to the recruitment industry norm. The findings showed that people stayed with the company for a number of reasons. One important factor was the sense of inclusion that most people felt. This finding was not un-expected. However, another common reason for staying was that respondents felt the company displayed a tolerance of differences: the environment encouraged and respected individuality. The survey planners had not expected this finding, but it gave a valuable insight into the company's culture and employer branding potential.

Another approach for seeking staff feedback is to give employees the chance to question senior management face-to-face about any issues that may be concerning them. One problem with this method is that staff can feel anxious about raising certain issues and intimidated by potential comeback (even if guarantees to the contrary are given) should they ask a more senior manager tricky questions. One way around this is to let staff prepare anonymous written questions. These can still be answered in the face-to-face group meeting, but the senior manager need never know who raised which question.

Organisations can also gain useful information by asking leavers why they decided to go, an idea we consider later in this chapter in the section on Exit Interviews.

Organisational flexibility

Throughout the process of re-recruiting employees, the organisation needs to have one eye to the future. Certain working practices may be acceptable to the majority of employees now, but what about in 18 months' time?

One issue that has attracted significant recent press comment and management attention is the problem of achieving a reasonable work–life balance. This is an issue for all employees, but seems particularly important to members of Generation X, as we considered in Chapter 2: The Candidate Agenda. How can employers try to help employees maintain a healthy home and social life, while maintaining high organisational performance?

In practice many employers will only adjust their policies when they are forced to by pressure of market forces – namely tough competition for talented people. In times of economic downturn, such policies may be temporarily put on the back-burner. However, adjusting working practices in order to retain a valuable staff member can save the organisation significant sums of money: advertising costs, recruitment agency fees, the cost of training the new recruit as well as any less easily measurable costs in terms of management time taken up in recruitment and reduced efficiency during the new recruit's learning curve.

Organisations that remain committed to experimenting with new ways of working and that continue to show concern for the challenge of achieving work–life balance should benefit from an enhanced employer brand. As we noted in Chapter 3: Strategies for Successful Recruitment, mobile telecommunications company KPN Orange in Belgium has made the creation of a fun and supportive working environment an essential part of its own employer brand, providing a shuttle transport service for employees and other services designed to help working families, such as child care and laundry services and banking facilities. Companies that develop such an approach enhance their chances of success when competing to recruit and retain staff in tight labour markets.

Good practice in terms of work–life balance can include:

- flexitime;
- four-day weeks;
- compressed working (such as nine-day fortnights);
- family days;
- term-time working;
- job shares;
- career breaks/sabbaticals;
- extended maternity leave;
- paternity leave;
- home-working;
- reduced hours;
- accruing time off in lieu.

Many policies are designed with a view to supporting employees trying to juggle the demands of work and family life. For example, flexitime working can enable working parents to share school runs, perhaps leaving the office early one day and coming in early the next. Some people may be attracted by the option of working extra hours in a day, but having a long weekend every fortnight – a potential effect of compressed working.

The key point about these policies is that they should give employees as much choice about how they work as possible. Cary Cooper, BUPA Professor of Organisational Psychology and Health at UMIST, believes that people want more autonomy over where and when they do their job. Greater autonomy is associated with reduced stress levels, which is good for employees and employers. Professor Cooper says: 'The more people are in control, the less they are going to get ill. So broadly speaking, organisations should have policies that say they will discuss flexible working options with every employee, not just managers. The options must be considered in the light of the particular role, and the individual has to be able to make a business case showing that his or her contribution to the business will not be adversely affected. If an employee wants to work in a central office 12 hours a day, five days a week, that's their business. But if they want a different kind of arrangement, they should be able to initiate that themselves.'

This is the bottom line: as long as the commercial and operational demands of the organisation can be met, why not consider different kinds of working arrangements? Employees should be encouraged to come up with their own suggested solutions; as long as they can make a convincing case that their solution will not impede the organisation's success or cause new problems for their colleagues, their ideas should be given a fair hearing.

Leading companies are taking steps to deal with the work–life balance issue. The Netherlands-based company Sara Lee/DE, part of the Chicago-based Sarah Lee Corporation, surveyed 100 of its top managers, of whom 70% said their work and personal lives were not in balance. Work–life balance problems were also identified as one of the top two issues raised in exit interviews. Sara Lee/DE has now committed to supporting employees in achieving an appropriate balance and recognises that this requires flexibility of thought and action on the part of the organisation. Its related policies have therefore been focusing on making work flexible, in terms of both place and time of working, and on offering support and back-up services.

When organisations do decide to promote work–life balance and introduce policies on the issue, there must be a firm commitment to make them work. This requires leadership from the top; if the top management are still working all hours and their cars are still seen to be in the car park later than everyone else's, then more junior managers will not feel encouraged to adjust their own behaviour. Linda Holbeche, director of research at Roffey Park, the executive education and research organisation, says that the existence or otherwise of HR policies on work–life balance is not necessarily what counts in changing working practices. 'Some organisations have zero in the way of policies around work–life balance, but managers have still come up with ingenious ways to enable people to work more flexibly, working different kinds of shifts or working from home,' she says. 'It's the managers who make it possible.'

Simple policies such as enabling staff to take sabbaticals can prove highly attractive and help to ensure that employees remain loyal. Established and successful businesses such as retailer Tesco recognise the potential benefits. Any member of staff employed for two years, and who has performed well, can take a general career break. Executives or junior directors can also take enhanced career breaks – which can last for more than 12 months – during which they return for four weeks a year in order to keep their skills current. The company believes the policy helps it to retain knowledge and talent in the business, while the cost of career breaks is far less than recruitment costs.[2]

As the economic climate has tightened, so some employers are seeing the offering of career breaks as a means to avoid making staff redundant. Consulting firm Accenture, for example, gave some of its 2001 graduate recruits this option, when it realised it did not immediately need all their potential labour.[3] We consider this concept as an alternative to redundancy in Chapter 18: Firing.

Persuading employees to stay

It will not be possible for an employer to meet all its employees' needs and expectations all the time. Sometimes an individual may look for a new job simply because they want a change of scene. In such cases, how much effort should you put into persuading someone who has just handed over a resignation letter to change their mind and tear it up?

The answer may lie partly in how big a shock the resignation is. In an ideal world, the organisation would have sound mentoring, coaching or appraisal systems in place that would provide an early warning of an individual's potential discontent. Assuming the individual is a valued member of the team, the employer could then take any steps possible to try and resolve the employee's concerns before they become serious enough to result in a resignation.

However, in the real world it is often difficult for line managers to keep closely in tune with the concerns and aspirations of all the members of their team. Therefore a resignation can quite easily and understandably come as a surprise.

Arguments in favour of trying hard to persuade the individual to stay would include the fact that recruitment is costly, time consuming and unpredictable. There is no guarantee that you will be able to find the kind of person you want, particularly in a tight labour market.

However, experience shows that the majority of people who are persuaded to stay start looking for another job again within a year. This is because there are usually several reasons behind an individual's decision to go elsewhere and it is difficult for the current employer to deal with all of them. In addition, we have noted the prevailing modern culture where moving between employers is increasingly expected. Indeed, some younger workers can start wondering what is wrong with colleagues who stay put in the same organisation for years.

As an employer facing a resignation notice, the sensible response is to discuss the reasons for the resignation. (This may take several questions: Why do you want to leave us? Now, what is the real reason you want to leave us?) If you want to try and keep this person and there seems to be an obvious solution, there is no harm in trying to do so.

If you are willing to make the attempt, do not waste time about it. If the leaver agrees that a 5% immediate pay rise and the potential to expand their staff development skills would persuade them to stay, get onto whoever necessary to find out if that is doable. Undertake to get a response that day if possible. The more seriously you treat the task of persuading the individual to stay, the more likely they are to believe that the organisation does value them, will try to accommodate their needs and that they could still have a challenging future inside it.

However, you must be honest about the chances of success. Say the leaver has been promised a 15% pay rise in their new job and this is essential to them. If you know that a missive has just come round putting an immediate pay freeze in place, you should not give the impression that your organisation can match the offer.

If the outcome is that the resignation stands, as far as possible try to ensure that the individual leaves with a positive impression of the organisation. You may want to headhunt them back again in a few years' time.

Notice periods and garden leave

When a high profile employee resigns organisations have to take a decision on how much notice they will require that individual to serve and whether there is any point in trying to delay their start date with the new employer.

The answer has to be considered in both commercial and legal terms. As far as the former is concerned, if the individual will be privy to confidential or strategic business information on an on-going basis, then it may be preferable to put them on 'garden leave' or let them go immediately. Either way, unless leaving early is expressly requested by the employee, you will generally need to pay off the employee by way of salary whilst they are 'in the garden' or through a termination package in lieu of notice. Otherwise, there are probably benefits in requiring the individual to serve out their notice period, which avoids any immediate staffing shortage. In addition, the individual can help determine the appropriate strategy for their replacement, whether a real recruitment need exists and if so, what the job description and candidate profile should be.

In terms of the length of the notice period, this will be established in the individual's employment contract. However, it is difficult for an employer to stop an employee leaving after giving a reasonable period of notice and, in any event, after three to six months. (This is something to consider when offering long notice periods in job contracts; they probably provide more benefit to the employee than the employer.) European law establishes that an individual is able to work for whomever he chooses and cannot be prevented from working for anyone else, unless there are very persuasive arguments. These would revolve around the employee joining a competitor and having access to confidential or strategic business information or customer relationships.

It may still be possible to delay the individual's start date with their new employer by putting them on garden leave. However, this possibility needs to be specified in the employment contract. Without that provision, as an employer you cannot stop the individual from coming into your office, with the risk that brings of confidential information being leaked. The only alternative is to allow the individual to leave without completing their notice period.

Another consideration for employers is whether there is any value in restrictive covenants. Many senior employees will have restrictive covenants written into their contracts which concern what the individual is or is not permitted to do once their employment with that organisation ceases. They may state that the employee is not permitted to work in certain market sectors, deal with or solicit clients or employees of the organisation, or work in a specified geographic area – all for a given period of time.

In practice, drafting restrictive covenants is a complex business and they must always be tailored to the particular individual's situation. If they are found to be unreasonable – perhaps because they state a year's duration for a non-compete covenant which is at the time or subsequently considered too long – then they may be unenforceable. Different covenants may require different time periods to be enforceable. For example, six months may be the maximum period for which a non-compete restrictive covenant can apply, but 12 months for non-solicitation in the same contract could be enforceable. Such covenants must also be deemed necessary to adequately protect the employer's legitimate business interests. Employers should always seek legal advice on such matters.

When considering the benefits of enforcing such contractual provisions, the employer should also bear in mind the potential negative impact on its reputation if it is seen to be acting harshly or unfairly, even if strictly correctly in the eyes of the law.

Exit interviews

Earlier in this chapter we considered the value to be gained from asking employees why they join, why they stay and why they leave. Exit interviews provide a framework in which to gather information on the leaving decision.

Many organisations do not bother to conduct exit interviews, and of those that do, many fail to make the most of them.

The most essential requirement for getting maximum value from leaving interviews is that an appropriate person be chosen as the interviewer. There is no point asking the leaver's line manager to be in charge of the exit interview. If the leaver has resigned because of that line manager, HR will never get to hear about it. A member of the HR department itself is the most appropriate person to host the exit interview.

One of the difficulties with exit interviews is that the leaver may not want to rock the boat. Say that the leaver does not get on with their line manager, and that personality clash has played a part in their decision to leave. This person may still need a reference from that line manager and not want to say anything that could jeopardise it.

Of course, the HR department can guarantee that anything the individual says will remain confidential. Even so, the leaver is unlikely to want to take the risk. Even if the leaver does tell the HR team in confidence something that they think requires follow-up action, how can they do this without revealing their source?

What the HR team can do is to try and be on the lookout for resignation patterns. If there is a sudden out flux from a particular department, maybe there is a problem with the line manager. However, you cannot jump to conclusions. It may just be that those people had all joined the organisation at about the same time and that they naturally all began to feel the need for new challenges around the same time as well.

Apart from reasons for leaving, the exit interview should focus on the leaver's time with the organisation. Potential lines of enquiry could include:

- How well were your initial expectations on joining the organisation met?
- What would you say has been the highlight of your time here?
- What have you found most challenging?
- How did your role change?
- How did your department change?
- What could have been done to make your experiences here even better?
- Is there any extra training you would have liked us to provide?
- How would you describe the organisation as an employer?
- What could have been done to persuade you to stay with us longer?
- Would you consider working for the organisation again in future?

The answers given can give useful insights into the reality of the employer brand, as seen from a departing employee's eyes. They can also give an indication of how well the organisation is meeting the expectations of employees and what more could be done to meet those expectations. The answers may also, indirectly, shed further light on the factors behind the individual's decision to resign.

Asking whether the individual would consider coming back in future opens the door to potential re-recruitment. If this person has performed well, then they could be a valuable asset again in future, particularly in the light of the extra experience they gain in the meantime. As we considered in Chapter 4: Alternative Sourcing, it is good practice to keep in touch with former employees, whether informally or through formal alumni networks. Maintaining contact in such ways makes it more likely that past leavers will one day return and rejoin the staff.

Chapter 18

Firing

The recruitment process is all about bringing new people into the organisation. However, it cannot be conducted effectively without an understanding of how the ending of employment relationships impacts on the organisation's reputation – its employer brand.

Employment contracts are most commonly terminated for one of three reasons: underperformance, misconduct or redundancy. Although the circumstances are very different, how an employer handles each situation has a similar impact on their reputation and employer brand.

The link between firing and hiring

As far as underperformance is concerned, most employers underestimate the importance of taking action when employees fail to meet expected achievement standards. The reality is that most people would rather work in an organisation that did not put up with sloppy work than one that tolerated it.

This is particularly true of high performers, the people who employers have most difficulty in recruiting. The most talented and able employees like to work in an environment that is full of other talented and able people; this is when creative sparks fly, when the most ambitious strategies can be drawn up and achieved.

Organisations develop reputations for the quality of their people; those reputations are impacted not just by the rigour of the selection process, but also by the effectiveness of the procedures for terminating the contracts of under-performing staff. In Chapter 3: Strategies for Successful Recruitment we considered the importance of coherent management practices for making an organisation attractive to candidates. That coherency must recognise the link between recruitment of the best and policies for weeding out under-performers.

There is also a link between firing and hiring when matters of misconduct and redundancy arise. In both cases, the employer must be at pains to do everything by the book. While the outside world may have limited sympathy with employees who have breached accepted company policies or committed some other form of misconduct, the employer still needs to act, and be seen to act, in a manner that is fair to everyone involved. This needs to be fully understood because a failure to act fairly or to provide a fair process when an employee has statutory rights (generally after one year of employment in the UK, as below) will automatically be deemed unfair by an Employment Tribunal, even if the underlying reasons are sound.

When making staff redundant, again the employer needs to act in a way that is seen as equitable. There are obviously legal issues involved. For example, the employer *must* consult with employees or their representatives where the company is above a certain size, but in any size of company it is advisable to enter into consultation with the selected group of employees. In this consultation process the employer must consider whether any alternative employment opportunities exist and set up fair criteria for selecting employees for redundancy. Only then should the decision on who will actually be made redundant be taken. Failure to do so could result, under UK law, in claims for unfair dismissal where employees have been with the organisation for at least one year; now that the cap on compensation has been raised to over £50,000 (unlimited in certain instances, such as sex and race discrimination), the downside is clear for all to see.

However, apart from avoiding unnecessary legal costs, it is just as important that the organisation develops and maintains a reputation as a fair and honest employer. There is no point building up your reputation by having the most advanced and effective recruitment processes possible, only to destroy that reputation by the way you treat those who have to leave.

Effective quality control

An organisation cannot hope to maintain high standards of performance by its employees without some key management practices. Above all the quality control approach, as applied to HR practices and employment issues, must be seen to be fair. If employees believe that the organisation does not treat all employees in the same way, or that some poor performers are allowed to fall through the monitoring net, then the system will never achieve the desired goal of encouraging top performance.

The HR department must therefore ensure that:

- required performance standards are communicated to all employees;
- effective systems are in place for monitoring performance;
- employees receive regular feedback on their own performance;
- disciplinary and other employment procedures for warning employees are well known;
- disciplinary and other procedures leading up to the termination of an employment contract are followed precisely.

Performance monitoring and feedback

No organisation that wants to create a high performance culture can do so without establishing clear performance standards, making sure all employees understand these standards, monitoring performance against those standards and giving feedback to individual employees.

The foundations for this approach lie in the competency frameworks drawn up for each role in the organisation. Then, when new joiners enter the organisation, they should be given a full explanation of the performance levels expected of them. Most employees joining a new company will focus their attention on any bonus plans and how their performance will impact on their final pay and benefits; employers should make sure that they are also aware of any performance-related downsides to their new employment contract.

As we considered in Chapter 17: Re-recruitment, appraisal systems are often used as the key mechanism for giving employees feedback on their performance, although too often line managers fail to give enough thought to the process. Furthermore, most appraisals take place once a year, an occurrence too infrequent to give employees really valuable information or to create strong momentum to improve their performance.

A more labour intensive approach is to set up a coaching or mentoring system, where employees receive regular one-to-one feedback, not just on their performance but also on the ways that their careers could develop within the organisation. Although such systems create more demands on the time of senior personnel acting as mentors, they can deliver good results in terms of helping individual staff to give of their best and remain committed to the organisation.

Clarity of procedures

If employers are to maintain effective quality control procedures, then they need to ensure that all employees understand what the procedures are when their performance is considered falling below desired standards. This may occur when an employee has acted in a way that requires potential disciplinary action, or when the organisation is running a form of 'tough love' quality control as considered in Chapter 3: Strategies for Successful Recruitment – terminating the contracts for the poorest performers on a cyclical basis.

Employees need to have a full understanding of how disciplinary and tough love procedures operate. It is then essential that the employer follows those procedures to the letter. If it does not, problems could arise in a number of ways. First, employees may lose any trust that the procedures will be followed correctly in future, thus weakening their effect on performance. Secondly, the employer's reputation will almost certainly be damaged in the employment marketplace as news of policy breaches becomes known. Thirdly, there could be legal repercussions. In UK law, for example, an employer could be found guilty of unfair dismissal if it has failed to act in accordance with its own procedures; if such procedures require one oral and two written warnings, then three oral and one written will not be sufficient. It is also advisable to review these policies from time to time in the light of recent experiences and changes in the law (including case law), to ensure they give the required degree of flexibility to act quickly if need be.

Where no procedures are set down, the employer could still face an unfair dismissal claim if it had inadequate appraisal systems in place, if it had failed to inform under-performing workers of their underperformance or had failed to issue any warnings to the employee. If such claims are upheld against the employer, that could lead to compensation payments, as well as a detrimental impact on the employer's reputation.

Handling the dismissal

The way in which the employer handles the process of terminating an employee's contract has a significant impact both on the morale of other staff and on its external reputation. If an employee is being dismissed because their performance has not reached expected standards, that does not mean the individual will not be liked by other staff and attract their sympathy. High flyers may appreciate working in an organisation that demands high standards and is prepared to take tough action to maintain them, but that does not mean they will tolerate unfair or unkind treatment of those who fail to make the grade.

Employers must therefore make an effort to break the bad news in as humane a manner as possible. The individual must be given clear reasons for the decision and an outline of what happens next: how long they have got to make alternative arrangements and any help or support that the employer can offer them. In addition, giving an employee time to come to terms with the situation and make alternative career plans will ensure minimal negative impact on the employer's reputation.

Ensuring that the dismissal process is handled fairly is also essential for easing the strain on those required to convey the news. No line manager enjoys having to dismiss a member of their staff. However, it helps if they know that the individual has been treated fairly and will be treated with respect during their notice period. There is no substitute for honesty and fairness.

As a final point, once a decision about dismissal has been taken, the individual concerned should be told as soon as is practicable. Sometimes organisations establish the custom of handling such matters on a certain day of the week, often a Friday. Perhaps the thinking behind this approach is that the individual will have the weekend to come to terms with the news. However, this method has little to recommend it. Say the decision is taken on Monday, the line manager charged with making the dismissal will have to carry the weight of that decision for the whole week.

Legal matters

In terms of the notice period given, employers need to ensure they are acting in a reasonable way. First of all, there are legal implications: employers in the UK, for example, who do not give the required notice (as set out in the individual's employment contract) could find themselves on the wrong end of a wrongful dismissal claim. This invariably will be coupled with an unfair dismissal claim if the employee has worked for the relevant qualifying period.

Similarly, employers need to ensure that they are not acting in any way that could be deemed discriminatory in terms of an employee's race or gender. For example, if a female member of staff is dismissed or made redundant because she is pregnant or on maternity leave, this is considered by UK law to be automatically an unfair dismissal and unlimited compensation may be payable.

Redundancy

Redundancy has become a common feature of the modern workplace. In their April 2001 research report, Redefining Redundancy, career consultancy Penna Sanders & Sydney found that almost 70% of employees surveyed across the UK had direct experience of redundancy – either personally or through friends and family.

Although there is now little stigma attached to being made redundant, it is still an unnerving experience for those involved. Therefore, when employers make staff redundant, they must still make an effort to treat employees sympathetically and give them time to adjust. Employers should also remember that an extra thousand pounds or so in redundancy payments can make a big difference to the individual involved, but have relatively little impact on the employer.

Terry Nolan, Senior Management Development Manager at Unilever, says: 'Once you have taken the tough decision, treat people as well as you can and with as much sympathy as you can. The key element is time. It's never easy, and sometimes the money helps, but what really helps is having the time to rebuild self-esteem, and then to rebuild a new career.'

Even though redundancies often happen to many employees at the same time, the impact on each individual should not be underestimated. Terry Nolan says: 'Whether you are dealing with a single factory manager, or a factory staff of 2000, it is vital to recognise that it is each individual who has lost his or her job; they have been fired in a unit of one. The effect on their family is measured in units of one. It's no comfort to them that there are 2000 other guys in the same position. They care about their kids, their family, their mortgage and the focus has to be on individual support.'

Considering alternatives

Employers are required by law to consider the existence of any alternative options before making staff redundant. These could include transferring staff into another part of the organisation or the possibility of retraining them.

Another option is to offer staff the chance to take an unpaid, or even paid, sabbatical for an agreed period. The employee's contract remains intact, except that their obligations to work, and often salary, are suspended or reduced. At the end of the sabbatical period, if there is no more need for redundancy, the individual can resume his or her work as before. If the situation has not changed, and there is still a need for redundancy, then the process of consultation and consideration of alternatives starts again. As far as the employee is concerned, the key advantage of the sabbatical is that it gives them an agreed period of time to find another job, with the possibility of eventually returning to their original employer if they are unsuccessful in their job search.

There may be some variations for senior employees, who may try to negotiate a new agreement whereby if there is no work for them after the sabbatical, they will receive an agreed sum in severance pay. Similarly, some employers may themselves want to establish a contractual position whereby employees can be made redundant immediately after returning from sabbatical if the situation has not changed in terms of the need for redundancy.

Whatever the details of the agreement, sabbaticals can give both employer and employee a breathing space before any actual redundancy terms come into effect.

Outplacement

Employers faced with making staff redundant, whether just one person or numerous individuals, may benefit from the services of an outplacement consultant.

What is outplacement?

The term outplacement refers to the service of advising individuals on how best to go about finding a new job and providing them with help for the different stages in the process. Within that broad basis, outplacement services can vary significantly, as does the fee to the employer.

Where a group of employees are all made redundant at the same time, the employer may arrange for a packaged service. This will enable the staff to use the outplacement specialist's services for a specified period at a fixed fee per head. The package usually includes a number of seminars on job-hunting topics, such as how employees can identify their skills, understanding the job market, CV preparation, how to complete application forms, how to write covering letters, networking techniques, preparing for interviews and general advice on how to manage the job search.

The redundant staff members will usually also be able to make use of the outplacement specialist's resources, such as office space, job vacancy databases, job-hunting reference material, PC and Internet access and perhaps typing services. The package may also include an amount of individual counselling sessions with a consultant, the aim being to provide tailored advice on running an effective job search. The outplacement services may also include personal finance, tax and investment advice, as well as psychometric testing and other practice sessions (such as being videoed during a mock interview).

The more senior the individual being made redundant, the more expensive the services generally become. This is because employers usually recognise that senior employees want more personal counselling and assistance. Where the departing executive is extremely senior, perhaps the chief executive or another board director, outplacement firms can provide open-ended services. This means they will continue to counsel and assist the former director until their career has taken off again. This kind of service can be extremely expensive – around £30,000 and up – but does significantly ease the pain for the departing executive.

Why use outplacement?

The main reason for paying for outplacement services is that redundant employees benefit from it. The Penna Sanders and Sydney research found that just a third of people made redundant had received any counselling or help from their employer in finding a new job. However, 45% thought that employers had a responsibility to help redundant staff find alternative employment. In other words, employees want their employers to help them cope with redundancy and outplacement is an effective way of doing so. Although the stigma attached to redundancy has declined, employees who go through the experience will probably still suffer some loss of esteem; morale boosting advice can be a big help in the immediate aftermath of being told you have lost your job.

There are several advantages from deciding to meet the cost of outplacement. Not only do the people facing redundancy have a source of support and advice, but the employees who are remaining behind also feel better about the situation. Experience shows that staff who stay on when their colleagues are made redundant feel a sense of guilt. This can affect their morale going forward and, inevitably, their performance. How much worse will they feel if those made redundant are effectively kicked out in the cold with no help whatsoever?

In addition, when an organisation has to make some staff redundant those remaining behind inevitably feel insecure themselves.

How do they know that there will not be another round of cut-backs or restructuring soon? It is likely that remaining employees will review their career options and perhaps start looking for a new job. However, if their current employer shows that it does what it can to help people who have to leave, then the staff staying behind will feel less threatened.

To help reassure staff, the employer should always try to be as clear and honest as possible in all communication with employees. For example, if you are confident that, because you have made deep cuts and numerous redundancies now there will be no further lay offs in future, you should say so clearly. If you cannot give this level of carte blanche reassurance, try to be as informative as you can. Perhaps there will be a review of the situation in six months' time. If so, tell your employees now that there will be no more redundancies for at least the next six months, and that you will try to avoid making any even then, depending on the economic climate. Stress that no one should be concerned about their immediate future with the organisation. Too often employers give no information at all because they do not feel absolutely sure about the future. However, an honest indication of the situation is far better than nothing.

Acting in such ways has the overall effect of reinforcing the organisation's reputation as a responsible employer. People accept that redundancy is a fact of life; they do not accept that employers can be gung ho about it. Acting in a caring and considerate way when making staff redundant, and being prepared to pay cash for support services, creates as positive an impression as is possible, given the circumstances.

Getting the best from outplacement

If you decide that engaging the services of an outplacement firm could be useful, follow best practice when making the appointment. Firms may specialise in certain areas. Some focus on top-end assignments. They can offer help and advice to people who have held the most senior, high profile roles, whose reputations may have taken a bashing before their departure. Other firms work with employees at all levels across all functions.

Clarify whether you want the outplacement specialist to assist with the initial stages of redundancy planning. Firms may be able to provide training on how to break the news, give advice on severance packages and on how to handle public relations in a way that minimises the reputational or commercial fall-out from the redundancies. They can also help with providing immediate counselling services to employees who have just been told the bad news. In general, the best results of the service will come from specifying precisely what you want and keeping the outplacement firm fully informed of your redundancy plans.

In some cases, perhaps where a relatively senior individual is being made redundant, it may be worth giving the individual a choice of outplacement provider. This could form part of the severance package, with the employer offering to pay a maximum contribution towards outplacement. The individual could then compare the services of a number of firms and choose the one that seems most appropriate to them. In this way, both the individual and the employer get the best value from the investment in outplacement support.

Notes

Preface

1. Nordström, K. & Ridderstråle, J. *Funky Business*. Pearson Education Ltd, London, 2000.

Chapter 1

1. Williams, M. Transfixed Assets. *People Management*, 3 August 2000.
2. Axelrod, E., Handfield-Jones, H. & Welsh, T. War for talent, part two. *The McKinsey Quarterly*, 2001 Number 2
3. *Ibid.*
4. Chambers, E., Foulon, M., Handfield-Jones, H., Hankin, S. & Michaels, E. The war for talent. *The McKinsey Quarterly*, 1998 Number 3.
5. See 2, above.
6. Tulgan, B. *Winning the Talent Wars*. Nicholas Brealey Publishing, London, 2001.
7. Donkin, R. *Blood, Sweat and Tears*. Texere LLC, New York/ London, 2001.
8. Handy, C. *The Age of Unreason*. Hutchinson, London, 1989.
9. Handy, C. *The Elephant and the Flea*. Hutchinson, London, 2001.
10. Handy, C. *The Hungry Spirit*. Hutchinson, London, 1997.
11. Tulgan, B. *Winning the Talent Wars*. Nicholas Brealey Publishing, London, 2001.
12. See 4, above.

Chapter 2

1. Nordström, K. & Ridderstråle, J. *Funky Business*. Pearson Education Ltd, London, 2000.
2. Grout, J. & Perrin, S. *Kickstart Your Career: The Complete Insider's Guide to Landing Your Ideal Job*. John Wiley, Chichester, 2002.
3. Tulgan, B. *Winning the Talent Wars*. Nicholas Brealey Publishing, London, 2001.
4. Rigby, R. Promiscuous managers. *Management Today*, May 2000.
5. (Conference round-up. No named author.) Generation Y: the rules of attraction. *People Management*, 12 July 2001.

6. Wylie, I. The wish list: millennial generation. *Guardian*, 13 October 2001.
7. *Ibid.*

Chapter 3

1. Dell, D., Ainspan, N., Bodenberg, T., Troy, K. & Hickey, J. *Engaging Employees through Your Brand.* The Conference Board, New York, 2001.
2. *Ibid.*
3. *Ibid.*
4. Eglin, R. Recruiting at the touch of a button. *The Sunday Times*, 30 September 2001.

Chapter 5

1. Handy, C. *The Elephant and the Flea.* Hutchinson, London, 2001.

Chapter 11

1. Grout, J. & Perrin, S. *Kickstart Your Career: The Complete Insider's Guide to Landing Your Ideal Job.* John Wiley, Chichester, 2002.

Chapter 12

1. Grout, J. & Perrin, S. *Kickstart Your Career: The Complete Insider's Guide to Landing Your Ideal Job,* John Wiley, Chichester, 2002.

Chapter 15

1. Grout, J. & Perrin, S. *Kickstart Your Career: The Complete Insider's Guide to Landing Your Ideal Job.* John Wiley, Chichester, 2002.
2. *Ibid.*

Chapter 17

1. Thompson, F. The wish list: IT and technology employers. *Guardian*, 13 October 2001.
2. Eglin, R. Career breaks can rejuvenate workers. *The Sunday Times*, 7 October 2001.
3. *Ibid.*

Index